BE MEI

STRONG

DURING

TOUGH

Times

A Motivational Guide on How to Reduce Stress,
Gain Self-Confidence and Thrive

MICHAEL DREW

To Charlotte, Matthew & Lucas

Table of Contents

CHAPTER 10:

Introduction

To experience peace does not mean that your life is always blissful. It means that you are capable of tapping into a blissful state of mind amidst the normal chaos of a hectic life.
–Jill Botte Taylor

Standing in the office pantry, waiting for the water to finish boiling, you contemplate the possible side effects of your fourth cup of coffee for the day. It's late and you can see the twinkling of the city lights outside. Hopefully, the caffeine will give you the boost you need to complete the final section of your report before any serious health concerns start to show up. You've been working all week on this project, and you just want it done and out of your life. Perhaps you have even developed a small disdain for the project. It's not the project's fault, it was just doing what projects do. But it found itself on your desk and has consumed the last four days of your life. But you know there's a job to be done and that you'll feel good when you're finished. As you hear the mechanical click of the kettle and the bubbling of the water as it boils, you bring your attention back to the real world and make yourself a cup of strong coffee. As you sit down at your cubicle, your boss walks past and says that there were some errors made on a report by a colleague and she needs you to fix it by tonight.

Your boss trusts you to do the job because you've shown that you can be a pretty meticulous worker, a trust you've come to find has its benefits and drawbacks. Before you can even take a sip of your hot coffee, your boss places the new report on your desk and says it should only take an hour or two. She walks away and leaves you frazzled. Two extra hours wouldn't be the end of the world if you weren't already staying an extra hour for your current report. You've been telling yourself the whole afternoon that you just need to focus on finishing by 6pm so you can get home in time for your partner's roast chicken. It's your favorite meal after a long day of work, and you just want to indulge on the couch watching a new Netflix show with your partner. For a few seconds, you feel overwhelmed and unprepared for this new task. You hadn't expected this turn of events and there's no chance you can say no to your boss.

This is an experience that many people have had in the working world. Whatever kind of work you do, whatever kind of office or working space you have, in every variation of this story, people have had to deal with an unpredictable world. Even if you're one of the lucky people that never have to stay late for work, you still need to navigate a rapidly developing and increasingly precarious world. Our technology is changing faster than we realize and questions about surveillance and monopoly aren't quite fast enough to keep up. The digital landscape that was once dominated by fringe sub-cultures is now becoming an everyday marketplace, while we have to figure out what to do with our investments in this volatile market. When we turn on the news there is always a tense situation between deeply polarized groups, whether at the international or individual level, threatening to disrupt an already disrupted world. Vitriol and division seem to be the new currency.

As we enter a 'post-COVID' world, we are doubting our essential systems and networks more than ever. Rising interest rates, spikes in oil and gas prices, power outages, overloaded hospitals, and political games that seem divorced from the reality of everyday people. All of this is playing out on a planet strained by pollution, and we're reminded all the time that we are teetering close to the edge of catastrophe. We live in a VUCA world: one that is Volatile, Uncertain, Complex, and Ambiguous. Not just at the global level but in our personal and professional lives. Sometimes it feels like living in our own heads is a VUCA world.

What many of us feel like we need is to be able to find some kind of peace in all this chaos, to be confident that we won't just unravel at the next sharp turn, and to ensure that when we take the time to enjoy the beautiful things that we have, we are fully present. This takes a mind that can weather the storm and be resilient. We experience external storms every day, like being asked to stay at the office when all we want is to go home or having to put two babies to sleep without exploding out of frustration. We also experience inner storms, when we tell ourselves that we aren't good enough or feel anxious and afraid of being in public. We sometimes have an immediate reaction to a situation and an emotion attached to it. It may feel like we can't control our reactions or emotions.

But that control, and that inner peace, is what this book is about. This book is an accumulation of knowledge and techniques, from multiple disciplines, backed by science and research, on how best to strengthen your mind and cope with a VUCA world. The past few years of the pandemic have made people realize how important resilience is, and many have taken their health and wellbeing more seriously than before. Mental strength is an important contribution to that conversation. It helps us take control and be intentional with what we spend our time and energy on. It makes sure that our thoughts and feelings don't just happen to us, but that we get to create new realities with our thoughts and feelings. In many ways, there is an untapped power in the mind to shape us and our surroundings.

This book is meant to give you tools to feel like you are more of an active player in your life. Your life is in story mode, and you have the power to pick up the controller and play. You may win a few rounds and lose a few, but you will build up your confidence in your ability to play. This doesn't mean that your life is a game, but it does mean that you can complete tasks and gain more experience to become better at being you. Along the way, you develop more self-awareness and self-knowledge. This not only allows you to be a better version of yourself, but turns you into a better person for others. Being able to handle the stresses of the world makes us less inwardly focused, and gives us the chance to take note of what's around us. This makes us a better partner, friend, sibling, parent, teacher, student, colleague, or leader.

The tools you will get from this book translate into workable lessons and habits for you to implement into your own life. You will learn how to increase your self-knowledge, and how to harness that to build your self-confidence. You will learn the power of gratitude and how it can free you from the negativity that clings to us, and why letting go of perfectionism is the key to progress. This book will teach you the importance of healthy eating and exercise, meditation and mindfulness, and visualization. It will also show you that the best way to tackle your goals is through small wins. At the end of taking these lessons in and practicing these habits, you will be a more self-aware, grateful, positive, healthy, balanced, and self-confident person. More importantly, you will be a person who is focused on progress, rather than being weighed down by negative self-talk and self-doubt.

Progress is important because none of these changes come quickly. You will strive towards them, and some of them may elude you. But trying is enough. Be patient with the process and take it all one step at a time. When everything we need in the physical world has become so convenient and instant, sometimes we expect things in our bodies and minds to be the same. Unfortunately, they aren't. And, arguably, that's a good thing. The rewarding feeling you get from accomplishing a goal that took time and effort is far richer than if you got it instantly. Many of the neural pathways that we rely on are built on anticipation and reward. We need to be able to work towards something to really feel good when we get it, or come close. Even better, there are ways to feel good while you are working towards the goal rather than waiting until you're at the finishing line.

Chapter 1 will start off by providing an overview of the benefits of mental strength and how this book seeks to give you tools for mental strength. Chapter 2 will stress the importance of self-knowledge as a core component of mental strength. Another core component, self-confidence, will be explored in Chapter 3 through the stories of people who struggled with self-doubt. Next, Chapter 4 will show you why gratitude is good for you. Chapter 5 will discuss the pitfalls of perfectionism and teach you to let go of the notion of perfection. Negativity and negative emotions will be discussed in Chapter 6, specifically how toxic they can be for your mind and body. The techniques discussed before and after Chapter 6 will be important in letting go of negativity.

Chapter 7 is all about eating and exercise, and the plethora of benefits that healthy eating and exercise provide. You will learn that there is a "second brain" that influences your thoughts, emotions, and biology, located in your gut. Sticking to health and wellbeing, Chapter 8 gives you tools on how to meditate and practice mindfulness, and why they are so important. A vital tool for success, visualization, will be the topic of Chapter 9. And finally, another tool for success, small wins, forms the focus of Chapter 10. These last two chapters are particularly relevant to you achieving your goals and implementing many of the skills the rest of the book presents.

Chapter 1:

WHY GET MENTALLY STRONG?

*Increasing the strength of our minds is the only way
to reduce the difficulty of life.*
–Mokokoma Mokhonoana

Mental strength can sometimes feel like an elusive thing. A particular ability that only those at the frontiers of battle, elite sports, geopolitical breaking points, and new business ventures call on because their responsibility and corresponding pressures demand it. However, mental strength is not about creating a killer mindset, it is about empowering our life with the ability to see through the fog of everyday war, and to be able to manage our thoughts to see the choices in front of us. Our thoughts determine so much in our lives; they shape our reality, forge our identity, set us down particular paths, and steer us along those paths. Our thoughts open doors to new opportunities by enabling us to see more choices in our lives.

A clouded, undisciplined, and unintentional mind can make poor and self-destructive choices. A clear, controlled, and intentional mind has the ability to make positive choices that set you up for the best possible outcomes. And in circumstances where those outcomes don't come to fruition as you hoped, a strong mind is able to accept the lesson and move on to the next pursuit. This book is written with you in mind, and specifically to share the lessons and proven techniques I have learned, so that you have the tools to build mental strength and fortitude to overcome the challenges in everyday life, especially during these unprecedented times.

The paths we walk in life are not going to be fun and games the whole way. By choice or circumstance, we move through a world of adversity just trying to make the best of it. Some moments may feel like a stroll down Disney's Main Street, and some may feel like a winding trail filled with obstacles descending slowly into Dante's Inferno. Both experiences, and all of those in between, warrant mental strength as a tool to navigate the ups and the downs. Mental strength isn't just about having hyper focus or ruthless ambition, or unbridled stoicism. It's about being able to find peace within the challenges you face, simply because you know there is always a choice to be made. In addition to that, mental strength allows for better stress management which has a significant positive effect on your health and ability to sustain healthy relationships.

The world around us has always been a stressful place, but it may feel like the current era is particularly volatile, uncertain, complex, and ambiguous (a VUCA world). Being able to manage our own stress so that it doesn't get out of hand and consume us is vital to living a healthier, more connected and fulfilled life. Mental strength gives way to mental clarity, meaning you won't be flustered as often. Whether your job is particularly high stakes or not, having the ability to make clear decisions and handle the conflict and curveballs is invaluable. This extends to all facets of your life; a clear mind makes relationships, personal decisions, health, wellbeing, and goal setting so much easier. Increased mental strength leads to increased confidence. Knowing you have the ability to handle adversity and make constructive decisions gives you more confidence to keep doing it. As you build your self confidence, you will start to build up your professional career, relationships, and personal life.

In doing so, you build up resilience. Resilience is the ability to bounce back from setbacks. You will experience many setbacks in life, everyone does. They can be crushing sometimes. It's normal to feel afraid of setbacks. However, this fear keeps many people from doing what they want to do, taking chances, making changes, and striving for more. The thing is, because setbacks are inevitable, they shouldn't frighten us. The best response you can have to a setback is to get right back up and keep going. You don't need to pretend it didn't happen; setbacks are often important lessons. Extract what you need to, and carry on. This is resilience. This helps you weather the storms of the outer and inner worlds. That resilience is often put to the test and strained in times of significant stress. That's why it's important to build up your resilience, and you build it up by letting yourself be knocked down. Every time you get back up, your resilience has strengthened. And, thus, our mental strength develops.

Mental strength can be broken up into four Cs: control, commitment, challenge, and confidence. This book touches on all four, and they are prevailing themes throughout. Having control ensures that life doesn't just happen to us, but that we are active players. We gain control from being aware of who we are, what we want, how we feel, and what is important to us. We can't control the world around us, but we can control how we engage with it. Commitment allows us to stay on track towards our goals. When everything around us may feel overwhelming, we are able to buckle down and stay committed to what we want. If your goal is to develop your mental strength, committing to that goal, even by taking small steps, is already a show of mental strength. When we commit to something we tell ourselves that we are stronger than the forces getting in our way.

Challenge is the part of you that aims high. It's the part that sets a goal and works towards achieving your personal best. To be high on the challenge scale makes you seek out new things, embrace discomfort, and see the world as a playground full of opportunities rather than threats. Without challenge, we fear failure and change. Confidence is the final C, and is the belief in yourself and your abilities. Confidence holds the four Cs together. Having confidence that you can set yourself a goal and stick to it is vital. Having control over your life comes from the confidence to do so. In turn, as you show yourself that you have control, you have commitment, and you seek challenges, our confidence grows. This book will show you how you can improve your confidence through daily habits.

Change Your Mindset to Change Your World

Mental strength enhances our ability to identify more choices and opportunities in life. To access this ability, we need to first look within ourselves and gain better self-knowledge. If our thoughts and, by extension, our minds can create our realities and propel us forward, then it would only be logical that we know who we are in order to do that. A lack of self-knowledge leaves you vulnerable to having the world happen to you, instead of you making things happen for yourself. If you don't know who you are, how can you strive for a clear path towards pursuing what you want, and head towards where you really want to be in life? Once we have self-knowledge, we can authoritatively answer those questions and make better decisions. And because we can change what we know about ourselves and therefore what we want, we can change the reality around us. There's great power in knowing yourself, and knowing that you can change and adapt.

Sometimes it's as simple as accepting who you really are. Simple, but not always easy. The world may be trying to tell you who you are or who you should be, or perhaps you've been telling yourself that you were someone else. Accepting you for you is a major step towards self-knowledge and it allows you to seek out and find better work, better relationships, better habits, and a better relationship with yourself. Handling a VUCA world is infinitely easier when you know yourself and what you want. Self-knowledge opens the right doors. When faced with stressful moments, tense encounters, or difficult environments, having self-knowledge allows you to find some peace in the chaos. You will know how you feel, what you want, and who you are, and this relieves the pressure of trying to figure out what the best response is.

Self-knowledge is something you can practice, it's not something that comes to you in a dream or through divine intervention. Simple daily or weekly habits will help you. Embracing solitude can provide an opportunity to be with yourself and your thoughts, and in the process develop a clearer sense of who you are and what motivates you. Solitude doesn't mean being alone all the time, it simply means intentionally making time to sit, lie, or walk without any distractions and observe your thoughts. Journaling is another easy daily task you can work into your schedule. Writing thoughts and feelings down may make them clearer and more succinct as our minds can become cluttered and disorganized. You may want to just write freely and transcribe whatever comes to mind. Or you may prefer more intentional writing prompted by particular goals; daily to-do lists, medium to long-term career goals, relationship goals, what made you happy or sad that day, what motivated you, what did you do that you want to do less of in the future.

Meditation and mindfulness are two brilliant mechanisms for self-knowledge. They encourage you to be present and observe your thoughts. Meditation often conjures up a very particular image, and many people think you have to have yogic levels of flexibility to sit on the floor under a lotus tree while burning incense in order to meditate. But meditation is just a particular kind of mindfulness practice. Being mindful is to be entirely present, and to observe the happenings right in front of you. When you notice your thoughts wandering away from the present moment, you gently and non-judgmentally bring them back to what you are doing. Mindfulness can be practiced while washing dishes, cooking, walking in the park, or at a dinner with a partner. It's about channeling your attention to whatever is happening in the moment. Doing so gives you a vantage point with which to observe your thoughts, behaviors, and emotions.

The McGill institute says: "As your mind creates obstacles in the way of self-knowledge, you will need to find ways around them" (McGill University, 2020). Your mind tends to create these obstacles as a means of self-preservation, which is why you have to be so intentional in your desire to move around them. You also don't need to rely entirely on yourself in this endeavor. Acknowledge that you have blind spots and ask someone who knows or at least experiences you on a regular basis for insight. A colleague, a friend, a family member, or a romantic partner are all going to have valuable knowledge about your behavior and how you present yourself to the world. Be receptive to the feedback they provide, and let it be yet another source of self-knowledge.

It's important to note that self-knowledge isn't a process of fine tuning all of your strengths and ambitions and ensuring that you have the best possible appraisals from those around you. It's not a performance review. You are a holistic, three-dimensional, and complex organism. To know yourself is to know the faults, the hypocrisies, the moral ambiguities, and all of the underdeveloped and unresolved parts of yourself. Embrace the negative aspects of yourself. You can obviously still take steps towards working to address them, especially if they are causing harm to yourself or others, but don't be afraid to look your negatives in the eye and accept that they are a part of you. Being able to do so, and not running away from the flawed parts of you, is integral to mental strength. Just as your mind creates obstacles to self-knowledge, life creates obstacles to your inner peace and confidence. A strong mind is able to find ways around those obstacles.

How to Use This Book

Every reader may have picked this book up for a slightly different reason, or may have slightly different needs and preferences. This is why the book is structured the way it is, you have the ability to head straight to the chapter that you're most interested in and circle back to the others at a later stage. I would recommend starting with Chapter 2 as, I'm sure you've gathered from the previous discussion, knowing yourself is an integral and relevant starting point to every person's journey. Chapter 2 will explore certain triggers that may weaken your mental strength. Recognizing what may be hindering your progress places you in a better position to face the adversity and challenges ubiquitous to human existence.

Each chapter begins with a quote that catapults you forward into the content and encapsulates the core message. Additionally, there are motivational stories dispersed throughout the chapters and sections that exemplify mental strength in differing contexts. At the end of each chapter there is a Strong Takeaways for Tough Times pop-up box that summarizes the main points made and serves as a quick refresher for you to return to while reading or from time to time.

As the name of this book suggests, my goal is to empower you with easy and actionable tools to help you be mentally strong during tough times. Just like each of our homes, there are areas that need mending and fortification against natural forces. The areas that need addressing all depend on our individual settings and environments. There is no one size fits all solution. That's why I have developed 10 Weatherproof Mind Practices that will be introduced at the end of each chapter, starting with this one. My hope is that through trying and internalizing the practices that apply to your needs, you will be able to start building a weatherproof mind that will be able to withstand the storms and harsh elements in tough times.

Strong Takeaways for Tough Times

- Mental strength empowers our life with the ability to see through the fog of everyday war and enables us to see more choices in front of us.

- It is your primary tool for managing stress and adversity. It facilitates clear decision-making and confidence building.

- The key to gaining sustainable mental strength is self-knowledge.

- Understanding the ideals and things that trigger positive and negative emotions in us, enables us to make sense of our world and empowers us with a new frame of mind to start reacting with positive and resilience.

Weatherproof Mind Practice #1:
First Principle Thinking

Take a few minutes to reflect on what benefits you wanted to gain from reading this book. Write them down and then rank them by importance to you, at this moment in time. These benefits could be expressed by a word, a feeling, or a phrase. Things like "Get stronger," "Feel calm," "Be confident," and even just "Happy," all work. The single most important thing here is that those words strike a strong resonance within you.

We all know that life happens, and sometimes we are taken away from a personal project sometimes. It's ok. Just circle back to those three lines, those three ideas. That is your motivation to keep going. It's your gift to yourself.

Chapter 2:

Uncover What Truly Drives You

Self-awareness is the ability to take an honest look at your life without any attachment to it being right or wrong, good or bad.
–Debbie Ford

To build your mental strength, it's worth knowing where the weak points are and how these may pose a risk to your mind's ability to handle different kinds of stress. Again, this is a practice of non-judgmentally taking note of where your weaknesses are, internally or externally, so as to make informed decisions about how to improve or adapt. Try to notice the voice in you that says there is a right way to be you or a correct way to live your life. Take note of the voice that may be saying you're doing it all wrong. These binaries often end up distracting you from the meaningful work you could be doing by getting you stuck in a loop of guilt and overcorrection. Being self-aware is an act of self-compassion. Knowing yourself is the first step towards self-acceptance.

The Importance of Self-Awareness

Self-awareness offers us a clearer lens through which to view the world. Without it, we tend to see the world through an opaque and narrow lens. We build up biases, aversions, traumas, and maladaptive cognitive patterns that distort how we experience and understand our reality. This is very normal, and to a degree makes us who we are. You are a conglomerate of your past experiences. But you are also the sole interpreter of those past experiences and, therefore, have the choice to let them cloud your vision or give you valuable perspective. Self-awareness is the foundation of mental strength. It helps you understand your strengths, weaknesses, emotions, personal convictions, and prejudices. These things contribute to your overall emotional intelligence. Equipped with self-awareness, it is easier to understand others and how they perceive you. This tends to make us more impartial, and more effective at directing our thoughts and behaviors towards a particular goal.

Trying to direct your life towards a particular goal without any firm grasp of who you are and what you value will be an aimless venture of trying to catch butterflies in the dark. You'll no doubt work up a sweat, but most likely have nothing to show for it in the end. Knowing your personality gives you the control and power to shape your reality. Being self-aware also allows you to explore the corners and nooks where your weaknesses lie, thus you know what needs work. Through self-awareness, we understand our 'why,' and, as expressed by Friedrich Nietzsche, when you know your 'why' you can endure almost any 'how.' As discussed in the previous chapter, self-knowledge grows from simple daily activities. What it requires is focused intentionality directed inwards. This often starts with an honest and objective look at yourself. Simple, but not easy.

Notice how you feel about situations you are in, what it is that matters to you in your current context and why. Be aware of the thoughts and feelings you have throughout the day, especially when those thoughts and feelings are more intense. Allow yourself to have those thoughts and feelings without judging yourself for having them. Contemplate your motivations, drives, and triggers. Think about what you are proud of, what personal achievements stand out and why. Your childhood is often a treasure trove of answers, so think back to the things that made you happy when you were a child. What has changed? Are you still doing the things that made you happy? Why, or why not? This can be a great opportunity to write it all down. You can definitely spend too much time trying to make sense of things in your head, and writing it down can provide some kind of release.

Other people can provide you with insight that you may not be in a position to get yourself. Ask the people around you to be more honest with you and actually listen to them. This is an exercise of ego management as much as it is one of self-awareness. Let your ego be bruised. Your ego's incessant need to maintain control is often the biggest obstacle to mental strength. As this is also about self-compassion, be mindful of the words you use to describe yourself. When talking to others, when talking to yourself, or when you're admonishing yourself for something you think you did wrong. The words you use on yourself help create your sense of self, if you're always telling yourself you're useless or lazy or unchangeable it won't be long before you actually listen. That's how you create your reality, and it's a far richer reality when you tell yourself you are capable, you are resilient, and you're still learning.

Self-awareness work involves a fair amount of introspection. This does entail structure and intention. Reflective questions can provide a particular direction to your introspection. Try these out:

- What have I learned recently?
- What have I struggled with recently?
- How could I react better to this the next time it happens?
- What do I want people to understand better about me?
- Are there any patterns in my thinking or behavior that I have noticed?
- What am I passionate about?
- What do I value most about myself?

You can work through these in your head at the end of the day or end of the week, or write them down in a journal and keep adding as time progresses. The latter will probably prove more effective when picking up patterns or monitoring changes.

Awareness of Your Environment

Self-awareness encompasses more than just an internal examination. You do not exist in a vacuum, divorced from your surroundings. You orbit other people and their realities, their traumas, and their influences. Getting to know yourself is to a large degree getting to know how the outside world has impacted you. So you will also need to evaluate the impact of your family and friends. The formative years of your childhood hold many answers to the question of who you are now. How your parents spoke to you, treated you, rewarded you, and punished you can often leave an indelible mark on your sense of self. For many people, there may be serious trauma that lies under the surface, and there may be great benefit to seeking professional assistance in exploring that trauma. If you feel comfortable doing it yourself, or doing it with your parents, family, and friends, then embrace it!

The relationship you had with your parents molds many of the relationships you have throughout your life, particularly romantic ones. You may come to terms with that relationship being toxic, or the relationship your parents had with each other being toxic. This will help you understand how you behave in your relationships, the patterns you may have fallen into without realizing it, and what it is you are looking for in companionship. Attachment theory is one of the most well-researched in psychology and describes how our adult relationships are informed by the relationship we had with our parents or primary caregiver. In many ways, we seek out the love that is most familiar to us from our childhoods. If we received a healthy kind of love, we are more likely to have a secure attachment style and our subsequent relationships are more likely to recreate this pattern. If the love we received was volatile or not dependable, we are more likely to have an anxious or avoidant attachment style that we will recreate throughout our lives, potentially to our detriment.

Love and relationships aren't just things that happen to us, we are equally actors in someone else's life. Learning how our past relationships; familial, romantic, platonic, or professional, have affected us teaches us how we are affecting others. Self-awareness is being cognizant of the effect we have on those around us. Are we the source of someone else's anxiety, heartbreak, or disappointment? Do others trust and rely on us? What value are we bringing to others' lives? The environment you grew up in has a huge impact. There may have been a lot of social isolation that made you independent and self-sufficient, but also made it more difficult to connect with and depend on people. Or you may have been surrounded by a whole network of people, leaving you with a healthy sense of community but with difficulty being alone. Families are almost never homogenous, and political polarization is a common theme in home life. You may have passively adopted the views of certain family members, uncritically letting them become part of your identity. Perhaps all the political tension left you with a sour taste in your mouth, now averse to conflict and debate.

These insights come to us as we reflect and attempt to find answers to the questions we ask ourselves. The realizations we have can alter the very course of our lives, forcing us to reconfigure who we think we are and what we value. There is absolutely nothing wrong with saying "I deserve better." Conversely, there is nothing wrong with your loved ones saying they deserve better from you. This kind of self-awareness work will often entail you having to work through these feelings and experiences with your loved ones. To better understand how your parents, siblings, or extended family have affected you, you may need to talk to them about it. To better understand what you expect from and what is expected from you in a romantic relationship, you will need to open up that dialogue. It may begin, however, with a similar kind of self-reflection that I discussed earlier. You may want to start by asking yourself specific questions, and then move on to asking your loved ones the same questions.

Questions like:

- Is there anything you have taken for granted in this relationship?
- What do you think it's like being in a relationship with you?
- How do you usually react when problems arise in this relationship?
- Are you expressing your love in your partner's love language?
- Do you treat others the way you want to be treated?

Moving on from relationships, the external environment is rife with events that affect us directly and indirectly. As technology and social media have rapidly advanced in the last few decades, we are living in a world more connected and visible than ever before. Although some argue that the quality of those connections have deteriorated, the fact remains that we are far more aware of global happenings and crises. This makes us more informed and perhaps empathetic global citizens, but it also floods our minds with external stressors. We now know what villagers in Myanmar are experiencing at the hands of the country's military, we know that major governments around the world are promising to reduce carbon emissions while discreetly investing millions in fossil fuels, we know the grief and distress that Ukrainian mothers are feeling as they walk through the ruins of their homes hours after Russian shelling, and we watch on as hate crimes against minorities are slowly on the rise in a time where freedom and equality are meant to be at all-time highs. Not only do we know these are happening, as they happen, but for the first time we are experiencing them live through phone cameras, live streams and tweets as the average individual has access to the internet.

It is not unusual for global atrocities and strife to affect your mental state, and for many it can be a serious cause of volatility, uncertainty, complexity, and ambiguity. These events are out of your control, and your brain isn't a fan of things out of its control. So not only do you have to deal with the uncertainty that may exist in your own sense of self and in your immediate micro world of relationships and career, but also the uncertainty from the macro geopolitical, socio-economic, and environmental order. It can be overwhelming. But that is exactly why mental strength is important. That is exactly why self-knowledge and self-awareness are important. You need to know yourself before you can have resilience. This has especially been put to the test in the last few years as a result of the global pandemic, the subsequent financial crisis, and the evolving post-COVID landscape. You may be feeling exhausted because of all of this global turbulence.

All of the external stressors are going to be obstacles to your mental strength, and at the same time they are opportunities to increase your mental strength. The best thing you can do is develop patience. Learning how to handle stress and volatility and anguish is not a sprint, it's often about taking small incremental steps towards progress. Even when it feels like the world around you is in a state of disaster, you still need to find the time to reflect, journal, be mindful, and practice the other small habits in this book. It probably won't be sustainable to incorporate all of them into your schedule at once, as this can increase the feelings of overwhelm. Choose one or two things that you would like to address or start practicing and get good at those. After that you can slowly move on to the next thing, and so on. This is vital because mental strength allows you to handle stress and keep going while juggling multiple balls as much as it allows you to be quiet with yourself, be present, and be patient. They're two sides of the same coin.

The ability to be still and take things slow is a symptom of control and clarity. Trying to rush through progress can be quite erratic, and it is often a consequence of a lack of emotional regulation. If you don't have an understanding or a firm grasp on your emotions, you are less likely to concentrate on one thing at a time and make slow progress. The main thing you will be focused on is feeling like you are doing something, feeling like you are making progress in order to quiet down the stressed and overwhelmed feelings. This often leads to unsustainable habits. Practice being kind to yourself while you're making progress. The process doesn't need to be rushed. If the words you use on yourself help create your reality, then practice positive self-talk. This is a form of self-compassion that recognizes that although you may be struggling at the moment, you will be okay. Saying positive things to yourself is connected to Cognitive Behavioral Therapy (CBT), a therapy technique in psychology used to balance the negative thoughts we have through internal dialogue.

There are plenty of examples of positive self-talk that you can use to help you cope, but the best ones are those catered specifically to you. Know what you are struggling with, where you want to be, and tell yourself that you will get there. Patience can be understood as a manifestation of self-awareness and self-acceptance, because it acknowledges the process and rejects the need to be perfect. Learning how to cope with external stressors is also a perfect opportunity for mindfulness. Practicing mindfulness, meditation, or any other relaxation technique that you enjoy will help you learn patience and stillness in the face of a VUCA environment.

Elizabeth Gilbert & Her Self-Discovery Journey

In today's world, there are many people who will find themselves in a perfectly respectable and stable life, having accomplished many of the things that they are told to accomplish, but with something missing. One of these people, as an example, may have an impressive office job that affords them a generous salary to fund their lifestyle, well-known and wealthy friends in the industry, an attractive partner, and a lovely home. This person may have found a successful career path and a comfortable home life that outsiders are quite jealous of. But this person may also struggle with the fact that they don't truly know who they are and what they want. This is what happened to Elizabeth Gilbert.

Elizabeth decided to take a hiatus from her regular life and pursue something greater to help her make sense of who she was and how she could get back the thing that was missing from her life. In a drastic move, she divorced her husband, was involved in an affair, and spent the next 12 months traveling on a journey of self-discovery. Along the way, Elizabeth explored all sorts of sights, sounds, and tastes that helped her gain perspective and come to terms with herself. She gained self-knowledge from the good things she experienced as well as the mistakes she made. Elizabeth's journeys became the subject of the book "Eat, Pray, Love," as she was a writer, and subsequently a movie of the same name.

Elizabeth's story is unique in that she was able to travel the world. You don't need to take a year off from your normal life and disappear into a different country every four months in order to gain more self-knowledge. Essentially, what Elizabeth did was take time away from her daily pressures and expectations to look inward and find clarity. That's something that anyone can do from anywhere. Through the process of self-reflection, you come to terms with your priorities. You will find what matters to you, not because someone or something has told you that it should matter, but because you have decided it does.

Sometimes we accumulate things that we know make us look good. A fancy job, a nice apartment, an attractive partner, and a lavish lifestyle. There is nothing wrong with wanting any of those things, just as long as they are for you and not for external validation. Once you have discovered what truly matters to you, you can begin the process of internalizing the shift in perception that will energize us along the journey of self-empowerment and self-improvement to gain the mental strength to handle the tough times in life.

Strong Takeaways for Tough Times

- Self-awareness is the foundation of mental strength.
- It is more than an awareness of your own thoughts and feelings, it is also an awareness of your surrounding environment and how it affects you.
- The first step towards better self-knowledge is to accept the real you, and the real world around you. Self-knowledge is our inner compass. It will help us navigate the changing world around us with self-assured purpose and intent.
- Our thoughts not only determine the paths that we take but also how we choose to act along those journeys. They open doors to new opportunities by enabling us to see more choices in our lives.
- If we change our mindset, we change our world.

Weatherproof Mind Practice #2:
Pain Point Scan

As I've outlined in this chapter, if you don't truly understand your drivers (what motivates you towards something) and stressors (what motivates you away from something), you cannot begin to build the mental muscles to lift you above the tough times. A simple way to approach this is by first referring to the top three reasons you picked up this book (your first principles), and then reflecting on them by asking yourself these three questions:

1.   Why are these things important to me?

2.   Who and what is preventing me from feeling this way? Is it due to personal history, circumstances or self-prescribed beliefs? These are your stressors. They can be people and situations.

3.   When do I feel those top three things? Who is there, where am I, what did I do? These are your drivers.

Try to view yourself from as objective of a position as possible; view yourself from the outside looking in. Now draw a large letter T on a piece of paper. Write your drivers on one side, and your stressors on the other. Congratulations! You have now completed your Pain Point Scan. When doing this exercise, it's always tempting to be expressive because these ideas trigger strong emotions. We will benefit immensely by keeping it as simple as possible. Try not to attach too much personal history to it. We just want to label it, and address it. Later in the book, we will want to circle back and deal with them in their own way.

In the meantime, I'd like you to think about how you can increase your exposure to your drivers. Are there any simple things you can do each day, at a specific time, say before or after work, that you could recreate the conditions of those drivers? Set yourself goals and steps to get there and ask for feedback from those around you in the driver column.

Chapter 3:

From Self-Doubt to Self-Confidence: Stories of Success

Successful people have fear, successful people have doubts, and successful people have worries. They just don't let these feelings stop them.
–T. Harv Eker

As a society, we tend to value successful people and aspire to be them. This can be a source of great motivation and inspiration; we see someone do something that is somewhat similar to what we want to do, and they become our blueprint. But we can also deify those same successful people and in the process forget that they struggle with insecurities and uncertainty. Trail blazing entrepreneurs still have moments of doubt and second guessing, even in their most successful endeavors. They too benefit from introspection and reflection in order to focus on what it is they want and value. In the process, they get a better sense of who they are and who they want to be. The rest of the chapter is dedicated to some of these stories of those who have found great success in what they do despite, and, perhaps, because of their self-doubt. The migration from self-doubt to self-confidence is likely to be one you will make multiple times throughout your life. Along the path there is knowledge to be found.

Do I Have to Be a Warrior?

Kickstarter has had a trajectory much like any other successful and pioneering tech startup of the last few decades. Recognised alongside contemporaries like Twitter, Snapchat, and Cloudflare as a leading startup back in 2013, Kickstarter serves as a crowdfunding platform for creators and creative projects. Beyond mere job creation, Kickstarter has invigorated the creative economy and made way for better collaboration. By many metrics, it has been a success. But its co-founder and once CEO, Yancey Strickler, wasn't reveling in its success as you might think. Yancey felt uneasy, plagued with anxiety and self-doubt over the direction of his company. With so many moving parts in an expanding enterprise, Yancey felt the pressure to keep breaking through barriers, reach new milestones, and maximize profit.

But this wasn't exactly what he set out to do originally. Yancey wanted Kickstarter to be a marketplace for creation and collaboration, not a well-oiled money machine. He saw the messaging around him, the media bandying war-like rhetoric to describe the world of competition, growth, and venture capital. He began to wonder if he needed to be a warrior in this economic battle to keep all the different components and stakeholders of Kickstarter happy. To stay ahead and not fail, did he need to become ruthlessly obsessed with squashing competitors and expanding profit in a game of success or death? Yancey knew that once you start playing that game it's a slippery slope to every choice being about money. Despite the uncertainty and doubt he felt, he didn't feel like he could express these feelings to anyone. Outwardly he professed that his company was doing well and making great gains but inside he felt terrified of being ostracized for not wanting eternal expansion and conquest.

Yancey found the calm in the turbulent seas of his anxiety and doubt by remembering what it was that he wanted to do. Kickstarter was about creation and collaboration, not destruction and competition. He reflected on what truly mattered to himself and his company, and importantly, he came to understand that it was those ideals that enabled Kickstarter to enjoy its early success and to stand out from the competition. Ultimately, that was what actually mattered. This doesn't mean that in order to find meaning and purpose you must become an outlier and go against the grain. It just means that when you are faced with challenges that seem to consume you, the greatest tool with which to tackle those challenges is self-awareness. If Yancey had forgotten what he valued, he may have caved and altered the very nature of his company. In a moment of weakness, he was nearly swayed by the aggressive marketing of competition, yet he came out of the experience more aware of what those weaknesses are. He knows what his emotional triggers are and why he feels vulnerable to them.

Yancey chose not to be a warrior; he chose not to join the war and maximize profit at the cost of his mission. The best choice in certain circumstances may very well be to hunker down and embody ruthless ambition to reach your goals, but as long as you know what you're doing and why. As long as you can confidently say, "I know what I want and I am choosing to get it," instead of going with someone else's flow because you haven't figured out your own internal compass.

Understand Yourself to Transform Your World

This is the advice that Rosalind Brewer gives to new recruits who are struggling to find their voice. Rosalind is the CEO of Walgreens Boots Alliance, a global pharmaceutical company, making her one of two black women CEOs of Fortune 500 companies. Before that, Rosalind was the COO of Starbucks and before that, the CEO of Sam's Club. Rosalind's leadership cannot be questioned, holding top positions at multiple companies with a variety of functions. Handling the pressure and demands of these positions is a gargantuan task in and of itself, and Rosalind must also navigate these spaces often as the only woman and person of color. But Rosalind has always had a sense of purpose and an intentional voice. So much so that she was suspended for it.

In third grade, Rosalind took it upon herself to show her teacher that there was in fact an easier way to solve a particular math problem on the board. Rosalind had older siblings and had picked up a few tricks that were more advanced than the third-grade method she was currently being taught. Instead of wasting her time with rudimentary and cumbersome solutions, she walked up to the board, picked up a piece of chalk, and began to show her math teacher the shortcut. Teachers aren't usually fans of being shown up by their students, let alone one that is 9 years old, and Rosalind was subsequently suspended for it. But Rosalind wasn't so much a troublemaker as she just wanted to have her voice heard. Anyone who has been through the normal schooling system knows that classrooms aren't always places for children's voices to be heard and taken seriously.

Rosalind has used her voice and her ambition to earn her some of the most coveted positions in corporate America. Coming from parents without a university or completed high school education, she had to work her way up from the bottom, often with the odds stacked against her. In these positions, Rosalind has been very intentional with the policies and goals she has spearheaded. She has initiated diversity training programs, racial bias training, and made it a point to hire people from different backgrounds who offer unique perspectives. Rosalind knows what she wants to do with her power and she knows what she values. She makes sure that her new recruits know why they're there, and she encourages them to use their voice. This comes from her learning the importance of being herself in her professional career.

Rosalind wasn't always confident in her voice or her role in the larger corporations she first worked at. She felt like no one cared about her input. In an attempt to be heard and seen, she overcorrected and began to emulate the corporate personality she thought would earn her respect. Rosalind says she tried to dress and act like all the men at work. But this wasn't her, and her loved ones knew this. Rosalind didn't feel comfortable performing this role, and decided instead to bring her whole self to work. The unique challenges she faces, perspectives she has, and societal position she occupies weren't things she wanted to mask for any reason. Rosalind reflected in order to focus on her purpose and her motivations. Without that, she may not have ever found her voice in her career and she may not have brought the unwavering focus on change and inclusivity that helped her stand out.

Don't Let Perfection Blind Your Purpose

One of the effects of certain beauty standards being projected to us via the media is that we can develop all sorts of insecurities and doubts when we start to compare ourselves to those standards. This is usually discussed in relation to women but has increasingly been recognized as an issue in men, particularly young boys. The desire to look a particular way and attain perfection can be crippling. This can result in distorted views of one's body and appearance and, for some, disordered eating. This was Caleb Followill's reality in his youth. Caleb is the lead singer of the highly talented and acclaimed band Kings of Leon that he formed with his brothers and cousin. Caleb has spoken about the extreme lengths he went to in order to look the way he wanted. His mission was to lose weight, and he would do pushups until he couldn't any longer and go running in a full tracksuit on sweltering days. The longing for perfection led to extreme behaviors and beliefs about himself.

This wasn't the only time he embraced the extreme; Caleb lived a quintessential rockstar life filled with alcohol, the wild road life, and drug induced hazes. Although his wild lifestyle interfered with the band for a good few years, he was able to develop a healthier relationship with himself and his own body image. Caleb became less obsessed with perfection and started to focus more on finding inner peace. It took him a while to address his substance abuse, but eventually settled into a significantly healthier and calmer life. The need to be perfect can hinder your ability to accept your mistakes and failings, which means there's almost no chance you're able to learn from them. Once you allow yourself to be imperfect, true self-acceptance begins.

Accepting the Past Is Letting Go of Its Baggage

Many of us may feel like we need to handle our stress and trauma by ourselves to get to a place of self-confidence. Being able to say, "I did it myself" is often seen as first prize. It is true that the kind of self-reflection, introspection, and mindfulness you should be practicing and the project of self-knowledge in general mostly has to come from within. But I have mentioned the importance of relying on those around you for perspective and feedback when you may be too close to see accurately. The same goes for sharing your stress and trauma; there can be value in feeling like there are others with a similar experience. It may make you feel less alone, or it may simply allow you to talk openly about what you've gone through. Hilary Swank is an advocate for this.

Hilary, now an award-winning and revered actress, grew up with her dad mostly being absent due to his service in the Air Force. Growing up with an absent father, despite the nature of his absence, was incredibly difficult. For years she felt like she was alone in her struggles. But once she began to share her story and share her insecurities, she realized that other people are going through the same thing. Whether they've had a similar upbringing or share the kinds of insecurities that, in Hilary's case, all women face while being in the public eye, sharing your battles helps you find confidence. Knowing that other people have the same kinds of stress and trauma helped take a load off of Hilary's shoulder, because her stress and trauma felt more manageable once she knew that many people have beat and continue to beat them.

This gave her the ability to turn her self-doubt into self-confidence through self-acceptance. Accepting herself, what she had gone through, and how it shaped her opened the door for self-awareness and self-confidence.

Quick Wins Build Self-Confidence

Venus Williams' story is unique not because she pushed herself to become one of the top athletes in tennis, competing in grand slam finals, but because she did it twice. Venus has been a dominant force in tennis for almost two decades; taking home seven Grand Slam titles, 14 Grand Slam doubles with her sister Serena Williams, and two Grand Slam mixed titles. Most of Venus' success was found in the early stages of her career, before her sister became an unstoppable champion. Until 2009, Venus had appeared in 14 Grand Slam finals in 12 years. However, after her Wimbledon win in 2008, her career took a turn. She had already been battling injuries throughout her career, but mostly remained at or near the top of her game despite the setbacks. A particularly serious wrist injury kept her from competing in some major tournaments, sidelining her.

She came back with an impressive two years of tennis in 2008 and 2009; making it to the Wimbledon final in both years and winning in the former, beating her sister in a Grand Slam final for the first time in seven years, then going on to win Olympic gold with her sister in the doubles followed by consistent doubles wins. But the injuries were just around the corner, and Venus had to stop mid-game due to a hip injury. Her 2010 season was marred by injuries, defeat, and an eventual diagnosis of Sjögren's syndrome, an autoimmune disease that left her fatigued and with muscle and joint pain. Venus still played here and there, and experienced some victories, but her seasons were inconsistent and turbulent. Eventually, she made her way back to two Grand Slam finals appearances in 2017. Although she lost both, it was the first time since 2009 that she had made it to a Grand Slam final.

It wasn't just the physical ailments holding Venus back, the pressure she put on herself to match her sister's performance was immense. Serena had taken the tennis world by storm, at the time and still recently dominating her opponents. Serena has racked up 23 Grand Slam titles in 33 finals appearances. Most of the times that the two sisters had played against each other in a final, Serena had won. This added to the pressure that Venus was feeling, and her self-doubt began to grow. However, instead of letting it consume her, she slowly worked her way back up to top form. Venus knew she couldn't just train herself into a stupor and walk back into a Grand Slam final. Since 2009 Venus has, despite her injuries and autoimmune disease, slowly been making progress in lower-level tournaments while accumulating wins. Her career hasn't been the same as it was before, but her work ethic shows that focusing on small steps at a time is far more sustainable than trying to do everything at once. Venus understands the value of small wins, and this shows patience.

Calm Your Inner Storm to Build a Weatherproof Mind

When discussing the trials, tribulations, and successes of the famous, it is easy to get the sense that they are where they are because of countless hours, godlike ambition, and unwavering focus. These are qualities we may want to emulate at different phases in our lives, and everyone should learn to harness their own superhuman ability to work and persevere. But you should know by now that true mental strength encompasses moments of calm, clarity, and careful prioritization. Jeff Weiner understands this more than most in his position. Jeff is the CEO of LinkedIn and facilitated Microsoft's $26.2 billion acquisition of it in 2016. Jeff is also a highly rated CEO with one of the highest employee ratings in the world. Sometimes it is odd to hear that leaders of massive tech empires, let alone any large business, can get almost universally positive feedback from the people that work for them. We are used to horror stories of bosses being more akin to slave drivers. But Jeff values compassion in the professional world above all else.

He wants to understand what motivates and inspires his employees, and he wants to understand what they are dealing with. Jeff's compassion extends to himself too, though, and he explains that one of the most important things anyone can do for a healthy and successful professional life is focus on the things that matter to you. Quite simply, Jeff emphasizes health, love, and time. Even as one of the leading CEOs in a highly competitive world of business and technology, Jeff knows that being mindful and finding peace are invaluable. His health is largely centered around meditation which gives him the ability to be present in the moment and observe his own thoughts in order to better understand them. Being present encourages Jeff to better appreciate what he has, and thus he practices gratitude as much as possible by contemplating or writing down the things he is grateful about.

Jeff is intentional with his mindfulness; he sets aside time to do nothing. He may fill it with meditation, but this time is also used for free thinking and creativity. One of the motivations is to simplify what it is that he and his company is good at. Spending time thinking about, amongst other things, what he can improve forces him to streamline and improve specific things rather than trying to do everything. He appreciates incremental progress and doing one thing at a time. This is an important antidote to the complexity of today's world, especially the world of one of tech's most powerful executives. It also makes him more intentional, something that flows into a regimented but sustainable daily routine that he practices daily. Meditation and mindfulness play a part, but so does exercise and family time. By finding more time to enjoy the things that matter, Jeff has found balance and calm in his success.

Strong Takeaways for Tough Times

- Know that other people are going through the same struggles as you. Even the most outwardly successful and confident celebrities have had to struggle with everyday issues of low self-esteem and self-doubt.
- Focusing on who you are and what you value is the key to self-awareness.
- Self-awareness is the key to self-confidence. Make time to do the things that you enjoy, and to do things that allow you to be present and mindful.

Weatherproof Mind Practice #3:
Mirror and Match

Go back to your Pain Point Scan and refer to your Stressors column. What are the specific events that have led you to think about yourself the way you do? Where does the story of you come from? From what you've read about the people in this chapter and how they overcame their self-confidence issues, is there a stressor or solution that resonates with you? If there is, what can you learn from their solution?

In the next chapter, we will explore the importance of gratitude and how it will help you welcome sustained positivity in your life.

Chapter 4:

ACCEPTANCE & GRATITUDE: SEARCH FOR AND EMBRACE POSITIVITY

Be thankful for what you have: you'll end up having more. If you concentrate on what you don't have you will never ever have enough.
— Oprah Winfrey

Improving your mental strength is a slow and deliberate process of constructing the best possible reality to experience the difficulties and challenges of life. You design your world to weather the storms of human existence without falling apart after heavy rainfall and thunderstorms. The process is like building a castle where every stone strengthens the overall structure. One of those stones, and the topic of this chapter, is positivity. Think about having to deal with the volatility, uncertainty, complexity, and ambiguity of the world while you are in a miserable and negative state of mind. Even if you have ample self-awareness and self-confidence, and you make the time to incorporate a lot of the healthy habits in your life that this book has and will still discuss, being in a negative space will still be a massive chink in your armour. For you, having self-awareness, self-knowledge, and a healthy lifestyle with daily habits may put you into a positive mindset and make you happier, but unfortunately, it's not always a given. There is however a more direct way to get you there: gratitude.

How Gratitude Affects Us

Gratitude is quite a paradox; we all know that it's important and yet it slips through most of our fingers. We become so focused on what we don't have that we forget what we do. Sometimes we get so used to what we have that we don't appreciate how it could all go away faster than we can comprehend. Our days are filled with 'please' and 'thank you' that is mostly said without much thought because they're just an important part of daily socialization. We say them because they're polite, but we don't always take the time to fully appreciate their essence. We don't always accept gratitude. When we do feel it, it's assumed to be a very visceral but fleeting emotion that may resurface again in an emotionally charged but admittedly rare situation. Maybe we wait for the feeling to come, wasting opportunities to create the feeling ourselves. But this isn't the best way to bring more gratitude into our lives, and it shows an underappreciation of the power of gratitude.

Instead of waiting for gratitude, we must practice gratitude. It must become a daily routine that can be done methodically and intentionally. That may sound like it will take the magic out of it and turn it into a chore, but it allows us to rethink our entire reality. The more we focus on the things we do have, the people we know, the places we get to go to, and all the sights, sounds, and smells we are able to experience, we stop focusing so much on what is missing. When we open our eyes to the wonders of the world and how lucky we are that we get to share in that wonder, it quietens the voices of negativity that we often end up directing at ourselves. And when we step out of that negative space, we see that we're not as attached to or determined by it. We get to be more. We get to live happier and more positive lives. This is again where the psychological approach of CBT is relevant. By changing your thoughts, you can change your behaviors. If you tell yourself that you're simply happy to be here, experiencing all of it, you will begin to feel it and act according to that feeling.

In fact, gratitude practices are well researched and supported by multiple scientific disciplines. Research suggests that practicing gratitude can leave people feeling happier and less depressed. The effect gratitude has on your brain is very tangible, and it shows that you have the power to reshape your reality into a better one. Psychologist Robert Emmons, one of the leading researchers on gratitude, highlights that gratitude gives us an affirmation that goodness exists in the world and acknowledges that that goodness often comes from things outside of ourselves. Gratitude makes us aware of all the beautiful gifts that the world gives us, and in turn, we start to broaden our field of vision beyond the self. Some sociologists think that gratitude is a driving force of human social bonds as it encourages us to repay kindness with kindness. This is supported by research into the evolutionary roots of gratitude, using chimpanzees, which suggests it was the basis of reciprocity and stronger relationships. So clearly gratitude is and has always been intrinsic to the human experience. In your attempt to place yourself in the best possible position to deal with life's stressors and turbulence, being happy, less depressed, and more aware of the good around you is crucial.

Researchers have also specifically investigated whether gratitude can help those struggling with poor mental health. Their study used university students who had signed up for counseling in relation to depression and anxiety concerns. Only one out of the three groups had to write gratitude letters throughout the study, and at the end of the study, that group's mental health had significantly improved compared to the other groups. Those that wrote gratitude letters used more positive language in their communication than the other groups. This shows how gratitude takes your attention away from the negatives and focuses it on the positive. It also suggests that when you use positive words and think positive thoughts, it can have a very real and measurable difference in your reality. Your world reflects your thoughts. You can build any world you want to.

Gratitude doesn't always need to be shared. Only a small percentage of the participants of the discussed study actually sent their letters, and there was no noticeable difference in happiness between those that did and those that didn't. So, when you think about gratitude as a practice, it can be done in the comfort of your own home to absolutely no audience. This is why daily practices like mindfulness and journaling are so useful, they don't require anyone else's participation and yet you will still experience a significant improvement. The reason that the practices need to be daily is that, much like any other health practice, the benefits take time. You will need to develop a routine to incorporate the little changes you need to make and stick to that routine until all the little changes become one massive shift. Little by little, a little becomes a lot. Just so you're certain that gratitude matters; when researchers looked at the brain activity of those that practiced gratitude, they found that there was increased activity in the medial prefrontal cortex of the brain compared to those that didn't practice gratitude. This effect was present three months after the initial study was done, showing the lasting effects of gratitude.

How to Practice Gratitude

Many of the ways to practice gratitude are similar to the self-awareness practices discussed in earlier chapters. I've reiterated that these practices should probably become daily or weekly habits to make them more manageable, sustainable, and effective. Journaling is a great start. Before bed, after the events of the day, sit down even for just five minutes and think about what you were grateful for that day. Write down the thing that you appreciated the most about your day or week. Or write down five things that you were grateful for. Remember to be specific and intentional with your journaling. Writing the same vague statement day after day won't have much of an effect. This is an opportunity to explore what makes you feel grateful and why. It's a learning opportunity. Saying you're grateful because your brother invited you over for dinner so you didn't have to cook after a long day is a great way to assess what it is that makes you feel grateful. The more specific you get, the more attuned you will become to the smaller or more obscure things you're grateful for. Again, this broadens your field of vision and opens yourself up to the world.

If you have the time and the literary inclination, write a gratitude letter. It can be addressed to a person that made your day special, a family member you feel deserves appreciation, or perhaps a concept like security and safety. You don't need to send the letter, but if you want to improve your feelings of gratitude and improve your relationships at the same time, it's probably a good idea to send the letters. If you don't want to keep a journal, or if you just don't have immediate access to it, you can still take the time to think about what you're grateful for. Think about the nice things that people did for you during the day, or the phone call you had with a friend, or the sunny weather that left you feeling energized, and say a mental "thank you." Meditation, mindfulness, and prayer are all great methods of gratitude practice. You can sit quietly and focus only on the things that you're grateful for, letting them occupy all of your attention. Be mindful of what you have and what others have given you, even during a task as simple as cooking or going for a walk. If you pray, include the things you are grateful for.

Although it's a daily practice, you can still mix it up and try new and innovative ways to give thanks. Drop the journaling if it doesn't feel like you and try placing sticky notes around your home, or fill a jar with gratitude notes, empty the jar at the end of the year and read the notes, or climb a mountain and scream what you're grateful for off the edge. People like novelty. It's also important to remember that these practices are still an effort. A lot of the techniques this book describes are simple, but not always easy. You need to stick with it for some time before you feel the effects, and be realistic about the process. You're trying to train a muscle, albeit a muscle of self-awareness, gratitude, and happiness, and so an awareness of the difficulties is essential. This is called mental contrasting, and it helps keep you optimistic about the benefits but realistic about the challenges. Mental contrasting is about longevity. You don't want to go all in and completely underestimate the difficulty of the process by focusing entirely on feeling better right away. You also don't want to become despondent when you don't see immediate progress. This is a method to ensure that you can stay on track for longer.

Camila Mendes:
How Gratitude Calmed Anxiety

A great example of the powerful effects of gratitude journaling is Camila Mendes. Camila is an actress known for playing Veronica Lodge on the TV show Riverdale. She has a massive fan base and a Teen Choice Award, both due to the show's popularity. She has developed friendships, and a relationship from the show, and being on it has been a dream come true. But, like many people in envious positions, she struggles with anxiety and feeling overwhelmed. One of her co-stars on Riverdale gave her a gratitude journal. A gratitude journal is basically a regular journal, with the expressed intention of writing down all of the things you're grateful for. Camila had been having difficulty feeling gratitude as she was preoccupied with her anxiety and found herself focused only on all the things that were overwhelming her. She didn't feel like she was in touch with the small things in her life that were worth celebrating. This left her feeling incredibly stressed and unsure of how to deal with it.

The journal she used was the perfect antidote to that chaos. It's a five-minute journal with specific prompts that get you writing about what you're grateful for. Camila found that the journaling was deeply cathartic, and she was able to find clarity through it. Being an entertainer brings with it a lifestyle that is inaccessible to most, and you shouldn't compare your life to that of a celebrity with a team of PR specialists, makeup and hair professionals, and exclusive resources. But their jobs do entail a level of pressure and stress. For the average person reading this, it's likely very easy to feel like you're drowning in responsibilities, expectations, and various forms of debt. There may be negatives in your life that you have to come to terms with. But once you've come to terms with them, move on. Don't dwell on them and let them become all you see. Journaling and focusing on all of the amazing positives present in your life changes the way you see the world and leaves you feeling happier and more positive. When trying to face the world's challenges with a strong mind, it's infinitely easier to do so from the point of happiness and positivity.

Strong Takeaways for Tough Times

- Mental strength is about finding peace within the challenges you face, simply because you know there is always a choice to be made. Choose positivity by embracing gratitude, it frees the shackles that hold us from living the life we know we deserve.

- Gratitude is a core human emotion that allows us to build healthier and stronger relationships, mainly because it focuses our attention outwards on all of the things that we have received.

- Accept, praise, and embrace every victory and beauty in life no matter how large or small. It shifts our attention away from the negatives and focuses our attention on the positivity of the world.

- Practicing gratitude is best done as a daily routine through mindfulness and journaling.

Weatherproof Mind Practice #4:
Name & Internalize the Good

Happiness can be achieved through gratitude, specifically practicing gratitude on a regular basis. It doesn't take much time, and when practiced regularly, it will start transforming your outlook and your overall mindset.

Set aside five minutes of your day before the start of your day and at the end of your day to name and internalize the good in your life. These could be as simple as your health, your partner, your children, your home, or your recent accomplishments at work or at play. Name them, and then feel the joy and your gratitude for having them in your life. You can say them in your mind, or you can write them down in a journal, whichever way you feel most comfortable. By naming and internalizing these positive feelings, you are acknowledging to yourself that you have achieved goodness, that you have positivity in your life, and that you are worthy of owning goodness in your mind, in your heart, and in the life around you.

This is a simple, but powerful habit that will slowly build your self-belief, your self-esteem, and your sense of accomplishment. Remember, what you are grateful for is deeply personal and is not to be compared with what you think you should have, or what you think your friends and neighbors have. This is not a competition, and it never will be. You control your mind, external projections have no place in this space. During that 5 minute period of grateful reflection, just note that it is your time, bask in it and internalize the positive vibes you feel. You will start to feel a wave of calm in your body. Carry that vibe with you through the day, and into your sleep. It will make a difference.

In the next chapter, we will discuss perfectionism and procrastination, and why "good enough" is sometimes a lot better than being perfect.

Chapter 5:

PROCRASTINATION & PERFECTION: FINDING THE MIDDLE GROUND

The most dangerous way we sabotage ourselves is by waiting for the perfect moment to begin. Nothing works perfectly the first time, or the first fifty times. Everything has a learning curve. The beginning is just that - a beginning. Surrender your desire to do it flawlessly on the first try. It's not possible. Learn to learn. Learn to fail. Learn to learn from failing.
–Veronika Tugaleva

Procrastination is often demonized in society. It's seen as something that the lazy and unmotivated do to avoid any kind of discomfort and effort that comes with work. Many of us procrastinate though, and when we do it can come with a sense of guilt. We feel guilty for not being productive, ambitious, and diligent. We're told subliminally that we should be all of these things all of the time, especially if we want to be successful. So, we tend to feel that we have let ourselves down by taking three hours to start an assignment, going for 15 walks to the kitchen to look for snacks when we have a report due, or rearranging our entire lounge space instead of going for a workout. For many people, we know we need to start the assignment, finish the report, or start working out, but our bodies and our brains end up in a battle of wills that leads us to fill the time with some meaningless activity. When we look back on the time we've spent watching seven episodes of a new show on Netflix instead of doing what we were supposed to do, it can result in a lot of guilt and negative self-talk about our productivity.

However, the way procrastination is understood could be deeply flawed. Procrastination is often a malfunction of perfectionism. Put differently, procrastination comes from a desire to be perfect plus the anxiety about not living up to that perfection. There are many people who want to be exceptional, whether in their professional or personal lives, but feel immense pressure to actually do so. The pressure can be debilitating, and the fear of non-perfection can keep perfectionists from ever starting their tasks. In their minds, consciously or not, there exists a choice; to start their task and risk failure or to not start at all and thus risk no failure. The choice need not be a particularly rational one, but the dilemmas we have in our heads are rarely rational. To them, they would rather not start a project than start and have it turn out to be anything less than perfect. Perfectionists have incredibly high standards and anything they do, especially if it is something important to them, must conform to that standard. When someone makes the choice to procrastinate, it's less about laziness and more about an aversion to non-perfection.

The pursuit of perfection then, is a massive obstacle to you and your goals. You may think that wanting to be perfect is an asset to goal realization, even a motivator. But that isn't always the case. You'll find that the desire to be perfect can thwart your progress because you end up more focused on the eventual outcome and not starting with small steps. Procrastinators will say that they can't find the motivation to do their work. They will then proceed to find the motivation to do anything and everything but work. Motivation is rarely the issue. Perfectionism is. When you let go of perfectionism, you are free to start the process knowing that you'll be okay if it isn't perfect. The key is to lower your standards, but not dispose of them altogether. You can still produce great quality work when you focus less on perfection, you'll just do so a little bit freer from the shackles of expectation and pressure. You may think that it's better not to try at all than to risk failure. But to fail is to learn. When you miss the opportunity to fail, you miss the opportunity to learn. Opportunities to learn are an unlimited resource in the world so you should never close the door on any of them. And in your pursuit to be better, stronger, and more resilient, failure is one of the strongest currencies in life's marketplace.

The Perils of Perfection

One of the difficulties of working towards perfection is that it doesn't really exist. Perfection is an ideal that you've created in your mind. It's not easy to achieve perfection because it's not easy to measure what perfection is. It's an intangible concept rather than a useful metric of performance. What you can measure is good enough. Where "perfect" becomes borderline obsessed with the outcome, "good enough" is focused on the small steps you need to take now to get to the outcome. Where perfection wants every aspect of the outcome to be airbrushed and streamlined, good enough focuses on the most important components of each task. Perfectionism extends beyond the individual tasks we are responsible for completing every day for our jobs. education, or otherwise. It bleeds into all facets of our life and identity. Perfectionism can be understood not as the striving for excellence but a way of life, almost a philosophy. But it's a way of life that renders us perpetually dissatisfied because our goal, perfection, is unattainable.

Perfectionism in its extreme form becomes a way to communicate your proficiency and prowess to others. Instead of being good enough or producing work that is good enough for yourself, you want the world to take note of your perfection. This is largely socially conditioned; ambition can turn to perfectionism when amplified by all of the social and popular media narratives around success and being better than everyone. In the same way that unrealistic beauty standards affect how you see your body, unrealistic perfection standards affect how you value yourself. We are bombarded with stories of successful people, particularly today in the tech world, and messages from those people regarding how hard we should be working to make sure we stand out. The hustle culture of Silicon Valley and Wall Street tells us to be more productive, more innovative, and more in tune with new trends. This has led to a kind of toxic productivity sentiment where people, especially younger people entering the workforce, are pushing themselves to work longer hours in more stressful jobs. That kind of work ethic isn't inherently a problem, but you need to know if it's worth it for you.

This is where self-awareness comes back into play. It's important to recognize when your standards are too high and when you are expecting too much of yourself. You need to be aware of how damaging perfectionism can be. Perfectionism can render us protected and guarded. The antidote to that is to be vulnerable and accept that perfect is an impossible ideal. If you want to follow the guidance of hustle culture gurus then that is your choice, but it can be a dangerous path if there is no balance. If you find yourself following that path but it's at odds with what you truly want or value, then choose to prioritize yourself and become acquainted with good enough. This is by no means a manifesto for settling into mediocrity; being good enough still achieves your goals by taking practical steps towards tangible goals. Once you've done that, you'll have more energy and resources to pursue more and replicate the process. Slowly, your confidence will build. You won't fear non-perfection and you won't feel paralyzed by every task put in front of you.

Developing the capacity to take small steps and embrace failure will challenge the procrastinating perfectionist's behavioral pattern of doing nothing. Hesitating and mulling over a project because it isn't perfect is the same as inertia. Make progress with your friend, and take steps forward. Making mistakes is always better than making no progress. One easy way to force yourself to take small steps and embrace imperfection is by setting a time limit within which to complete a task. Whether or not you think that the task has been completed to the highest standard of your own internal perfection compass, when the time stops, you stop. You will need to start small, as trying to complete too much within too little time will bring you straight back to square one of being overwhelmed. Some prominent thinkers on this topic encourage people to make small mistakes and be a bit more spontaneous. They suggest sending an email without proofreading it or taking a bit less time to prepare for a presentation you know you can handle. These are ways to disrupt perfection and show us that the world will not crumble around us if something we do is not perfect. It also shows us that our value does not diminish because of non-perfection and, subsequently, our value is not determined by perfection.

You can practice intentional non-perfection in low-stakes environments that don't require you to put in maximal effort. In cases where you do need to perform at your best, something to strive towards instead of perfection is meticulousness. That is, showing great attention to detail. When you hone in on the important tasks that need to be completed, they may require a certain level of meticulousness; ensuring that what you need to do is done with care and precision. But don't equate being meticulous with perfection. As we've discussed, the latter is fueled by fear of failure, mistakes, and negative evaluations from others and yourself. You can accurately answer the question when you ask yourself "Was I meticulous enough?" "Did my assignment cover the three topics that it set out to?" and "Did I do my best?". The question that can never be answered about your work or yourself, in general, is "Did I achieve perfection?". And it is the fact that it can never be answered that leaves you feeling dissatisfied, disappointed, disheartened, and in many cases, depressed, anxious, and avoidant.

Gwenyth Paltrow: The Perfection Trap

One of the worst things about perfectionism is that it can distract you from what actually matters. When we have an idea of perfectionism in our heads, we tend to focus, almost obsessively, on achieving it. But very often it frustrates the process of us achieving our goals rather than aiding it. Gwenyth Paltrow admits that she was driven by a misguided notion of perfection for a big part of her career, especially in her own brand. Perfectionism left her more afraid of being a failure in other people's eyes than motivated to do what she truly wanted. This was exacerbated by the fact that Gwenyth was in the public eye and so felt the pressure to always present as perfect in order to avoid any kind of backlash. In her new health and beauty brand, she maintained an incredibly high standard that made work quite difficult for her employees. Although Gwenyth wants to produce the best product that she can, her perfectionism could at times hinder her from progress but focusing on things that don't really matter.

The average person reading this book doesn't have a massive platform, millions of fans, or harsh media critics to deal with. They also may struggle with perfectionism but not intense anxiety. But the core message of this story is to recognize how much of an impact your desire for perfection can be, and to be open and vulnerable about it. Your weaknesses can become a strength when you accept and own them. It's important to have self-awareness about your perfection and its influence on your sense of self. One of the best ways to develop a healthier relationship with your perfectionism and anxiety is to be open about it. You don't have to suffer in silence and feel like you're alone on this path. Talk about your desire to be perfect and you may realize how unattainable that is. Open up about your fear of failure and you may discover that there is a way to break up your task into bite-sized chunks. Discuss your anxiety and you may notice how many other people resonate with you. Accept that you may not have a grasp on your perfectionism or anxiety yet, and that is okay.

Strong Takeaways for Tough Times

- Perfectionism is a projection in your mind, it is not your objective or your goal.
- Perfectionism gets in the way of progress by procrastination.
- Focus on the single most important objective of your task, rather than overthink the process. This will help you get more done and relieve you of the pressure that eats away at your confidence.

Weatherproof Mind Practice #5: Chunking Tasks

Perfectionism and procrastination usually kick in at the start of the project. They also both start with the question, "How am I going to do this." The difference is the reaction–the project scope is either magnified or granulated. To disrupt this mindset, try looking at a task or project in terms of chunks. Just like you won't gulp your meal in one big chomp, you cut it up into bite-sized bits. The thinking is similar here, but what I suggest you try is to think about your task or goal in this way:

- Focus on your single most important objective. If you are preparing a report of some kind, define the purpose of the report—is it to sell a product or detail workflows? Your audience must have a key focus, or your department must have a key message to relay. Keep this in mind, and then break down your tasks into bite-sized chunks, ensuring that each chunk is easily manageable. The key is to get the job done, and not to focus anymore on the process or the formatting.

- Next, assign yourself an allotted period of time to each task. If you have one hour to complete a task, try breaking down your work into 15 to 20-minute chunks by setting a timer. Once the timer buzzes, take a one-minute breather and review what you've done. The timer will unconsciously give you a sense of urgency to get things done, rather than overthink how you can improve on a work in progress.

This can easily be applied to your personal life as well. Try applying it to exercising, or learning a new hobby or instrument.

The method will help alleviate a lot of the stress and self-expectations when we start to see how a task can be tackled in quick succession.

In the next chapter, we'll circle back to your stressors and find out how we can let go of negativity in our life.

Chapter 6:

RESENTMENT & JEALOUSY: LETTING NEGATIVITY GO

Dwelling on the negative simply contributes to its power.
–Shirley MacLaine

R esentment and jealousy are some of the most corrosive emotions that humans experience, and they can eat away at your confidence, peace, and sense of self. Despite how bad for our health these negative emotions can be, they're really difficult to get rid of. Negative emotions can stick to you like glue, while positive emotions can often be slippery and difficult to hold. Envy is one such negative emotion and Aristotle described it as the pain we feel when we see the good fortune of others. Negative emotions in general, but especially envy, can do exactly that: create pain. In a world dominated by social media, the facade of happiness that social media propagates, and the culture of always wanting and being more, it's no surprise that envy is so ubiquitous. A study published in the Journal of Basic and Applied Social Psychology finds that more than three-quarters of study participants had experienced envy within the last year. The effects of the culture of more fall disproportionately on younger people, with young adults experiencing the most envy (Kelkar, 2021).

In the study, the feeling of envy declined with age, but the study still shows that the feeling is experienced by many people. In fact, envy, jealousy, resentment, and many more negative and corrosive emotions are experienced by the vast majority of people. But the problem isn't just experiencing the emotion, it would be almost impossible to rid yourself of every single negative emotion because emotions by nature are impulsive and reflexive. Instead, the problem is our tendency to hold onto the negative emotions and continuously experience them in a loop. Holding onto negative emotions long after the event that triggered them has ended is what turns the feeling toxic. The emotions we experience stem from and subsequently affect our brains, and our brains control things like the nervous system. To constantly feel negative emotions and think negative thoughts can seriously affect all of those systems by keeping them in a state of stress. Negative emotions aren't meant to take up permanent residence in our brains, they're only meant to be wayward visitors that leave the next morning.

What Negativity Does to You and How to Move Past It

The negativity we experience puts us in a fight-or-flight mode as our internal systems become stressed. This is particularly true if there is an associated feeling of anxiety. To our brains, that negativity is seen as a threat, and because we have evolved to avoid threats as a means to survive, the brain's response is to release cortisol into the blood which increases focus and alertness. This stress response is important to our lives and can be a very beneficial thing. In many ways, we need that rush of cortisol and the focus and alertness that comes with it. But when we dwell on the negative and remain in a state of stress, our brains keep releasing cortisol beyond what we actually need. As a result, our health suffers; it can slow digestion and reduce our bodies' ability to fight inflammation. We may develop a host of physical ailments from chronic stress such as headaches, chest pain, fatigue, sleep problems and more. This then starts to negatively affect our mental health, leaving us at greater risk of anxiety and/or depression.

Experiencing that much internal toxicity can make you behave in toxic ways externally. You can become pessimistic, self-defeating, and hopeless. People around you may find it increasingly difficult to deal with you and the tasks that you are responsible for may become overly burdensome. Being in that space can have detrimental effects on your personal and professional relationships. So how do you get out of it? One of the best ways to do this was discussed in the previous chapter: gratitude. Practicing gratitude reframes your perspective by focusing on the positive and minimizing the negative. Reframing your perspective against the bigger picture also helps. When you zero in on something that you don't like or causes you anguish, negative emotions can develop. So, take a step back, think about the bigger picture, and try to take note of how insignificant that anguish might actually be in the grand scheme of your goals and motivations.

A change of perspective allows you to shift away from the negative views you have about yourself or the world. One thing that helps you shift your perspective is surrounding yourself with positive people. The company you keep can play a massive role in your outlook on life and if you're surrounded by negative people, or you surround yourself with your own negative thoughts, you're not likely to experience any other way of looking at the world. If you are surrounded by positivity, your own negativity is more likely to be challenged. This means you should prioritize people who are supportive, optimistic, and happy with themselves. Just as you could become toxic if you wallow in your negative emotions for too long, so could you be associating with toxic people that are starting to rub off on you. It's important to set boundaries so your peace isn't infringed upon by others. This means walking away when someone has stepped over those boundaries and is bringing you down.

Boundaries include not engaging in an argument with someone who is just trying to win without even listening to you, not getting sucked into someone's negativity by letting them complain to you all the time, or simply not allowing yourself to get too emotionally invested in them. It's not about being cold or neglectful, rather it's about limiting the potential negative impact they may have on your life. Surrounding yourself with negativity includes the kinds of movies, music, and art that you consume. Try listening to happier and calmer music for a change. Watch happier and calmer movies. Avoid listening to the news all day every day. Read books that inspire you. Your negativity is confirmed by the things you consume, and if everything you consume is negative you will just keep believing that it is reflective of the world in general.

To avoid becoming a chronic complainer, try to focus more on solutions than problems. Once you identify an issue, spend the time and energy to figure out what you can do about it rather than how awful it is. This will make you more proactive and less likely to hold onto the negative emotions that may flow from the problem. It helps to be more solution oriented in your work, but it's also a massive benefit in your personal life. If there's a problem in one of your relationships, find the best way to address it and move forward. If you are experiencing a negative emotion, identify the steps you could be taking to focus on positivity. When there may not be a clear solution to the problem, that is okay, too. The benefit of having mental strength is that you're able to deal with those problems that just won't go away by not attaching yourself to them. Obstacles are normal, but many of them are not as big as your minds tell you they are.

Be active. There are a host of benefits from exercise and activity that many of us neglect to appreciate. It might be that we've never been the sportiest person, or that we have a demanding office job, or that we just feel too lazy and unmotivated. Regardless, make time for exercise. Even if it is a short walk around the block, some light skipping, swimming a few laps, or whatever comes easiest. Exercise releases endorphins that improve our mood and it is vital for the health and functioning of our bodies. Good health can also be practiced through meditation, which by now you must realize should be an important part of your routine. Meditation lets us observe our emotions, rather than to be consumed by them. And when we feel bad without quite knowing why, meditation may help us find the root cause as we observe the feeling. A final but incredibly important component to health is sleep. When you are feeling overwhelmed by negative emotions, recognize how it may be affecting your sleep and try to get more rest. Sleep deprivation can heighten the stress you may already be feeling.

It's important to touch on the idea of creating the conditions for your success here. In letting negativity go, one aspect of that is creating a more positive environment around you. Surrounding yourself with positivity through music, movies, people, and other things you enjoy. That's one way to hack your external environment, but you may also want to try fixing up your immediate environment. This is connected to the reshaping of your reality, but here you're doing it by changing your immediate world. Research has shown that strong-willed people don't spend that much time resisting urges and impulses. One would think that that is exactly what they do, why else would they be strong-willed? The reality is that they don't even invite those temptations into their lives in the first place.

They know how tempting the impulse is, so they avoid it instead of having to fight it. This can be applied to the temptation for a packet of cookies, a glass of wine, a movie that seems more interesting than the work you need to do, and so on. But it's also relevant for negativity. Instead of having to fight negativity every day, make sure that it doesn't show up in the first place. Tweak your environment to have as little negativity as possible. There will still be days where negativity will show up, just like there will be days where you indulge in your favorite late night chocolate bar. But you shouldn't be confronted with them all the time. That is what wears you down and makes you fold. So, if your environment is catered towards positivity, you won't spend as much time fighting negativity. And, you will start to feel more of the positivity because, as we've discussed, you can create a different reality through exposure.

An easy way to create the conditions for less temptation, or build your will power, is to have reminders. This is called 'stimulus control': keeping things around you to remind you of your goals. Again, this can work with daily habits like skipping as you can leave your skipping rope out on your door handle to remind you to skip, but it can work with positivity. You can put a happy song as your ringtone or alarm, write positive affirmations on sticky notes that you leave around your house, or set a reminder on your phone that tells you to think about something that made you happy. Avoiding negativity can be framed better as inviting positivity. So, treat that as a daily habit. Add these habits into your routine or put them on a calendar. Many people fail at their goals because they simply forget. If you're used to being in a negative space, you may stay there simply because it's become second nature and you forget to avoid it.

You may need to map out ways to avoid negativity and do activities that make you feel better. Wake up a little earlier to make time for a run, during your lunch try eating outside in the sun, make a habit out of thinking of a solution every time you think of a problem, or offer a solution to a friend when they tell you about a problem. Although you may want to do that last one in your head as it can be off-putting when someone just wants you to listen.

Finally, work on building that conducive environment through inspiration. We spend so much time looking at screens, so why not put something motivational on your screensaver? Or change your wallpaper to a picture of something that makes you feel good. Every time you look at it, even if you don't notice, you're subconsciously taking note of the positivity. Your environment must make it as easy as possible to avoid temptations.

Emily Blunt:
Letting Go to Move Ahead

Letting go of negativity allows you to focus on the things that matter. Oftentimes, your negativity is the thing holding you back from discovering what you're good at and finding happiness. A great example of this is Emily Blunt. Emily is now a successful and revered actress with an illustrious career. But her acting journey began with a crippling stutter that traumatized her for years. Emily struggled with a stutter in her early teen years that she was often made fun of and embarrassed about. Kids would laugh at her and some teachers would shout at her for the way she spoke.

One teacher, however, noticed that Emily was quite good at doing accents and weird voices. This teacher also noticed that when Emily was doing the accents and voices, her stutter disappeared. Emily was encouraged to audition for the school play as a means to do all of her voices and work on her stutter, for which she got the part and fell in love with acting. Emily Blunt has since worked with some of the biggest names in the acting world, getting one of her first gigs alongside Dame Judi Dench when she was 18.

Emily was lucky that she had a teacher to encourage her as a child, but her story shows that when you let go of the negativity that has plagued you, possibilities and opportunities open up. Emily let go of the insecurity she felt from her stutter and stopped caring about what others thought of her. She found what she was passionate about and focused all her attention and energy on mastering her craft. You will never know what kind of doors may be open to you when you are stuck in your own negativity.

Negativity can hamper your creativity. David Lynch, one of the most prolific film directors, says that negativity is the enemy of creativity. Emily might not have found her passion if she let her negativity kill her creativity. Your creativity must be protected, regardless of your profession or passions.

Strong Takeaways for Tough Times

- Positivity begets progressivity. You have the power to reshape your reality into a better one. Use your power to accept yourself, love yourself, and let go of your stressors.

- Don't get weighed down by what you think other people are thinking. Focus on how you want to think and feel instead. That is what will matter at the end of the day.

- Letting go of negativity doesn't have to be difficult. Start by associating yourself with positive vibes through people, music, positive social posts, and nature.

Weatherproof Mind Practice #6:
Positivity Time-Outs (PTO)

Oftentimes, we get so drowned out by external demands—whether they be from our work, family, or social obligations—that we often neglect our own wellbeing. Finding time to be alone to do something entirely for ourselves can deliver powerful benefits by uplifting our soul.

• Pick one activity that you can enjoy by yourself on a regular basis. This could be anything from a walk in the park, yoga, listening to music, or engaging in a hobby such as playing an instrument or working on a craft.

• Schedule this time in your diary every day, and commit to this Positivity Time-Out as an investment in your well-being. By focusing on yourself, you are separating yourself from any negativity around you, and fortifying your mindset with the belief that you deserve happiness, peace, and wellness.

• If you can't afford to set a long block of time each day, try introducing mini PTO's. They could be before work, during your lunch break, or after work. Make sure that these activities contribute to your health and inner calm, so that you are building a positive daily habit.

In the next chapter, we'll discover how your physical health plays a bigger role than you might think in building your mental strength.

Chapter 7:

EXERCISE & EAT RIGHT: BOOSTING YOUR BRAIN

Movement is a medicine for creating change in a person's physical, emotional and mental states.
—Carol Welch

Many of us think, because we've been told for most of our lives, that the brain is the central control system within the body. Your brain, through its neural system, controls your emotions, your pain perception, stress systems, and a wide range of other bodily functions. While this isn't wrong, emerging scientific discoveries have shown that there is a second system that can have a massive impact on these things, and can sometimes exert control over the brain's neural system. This is the gut microbiome. Humans are mostly bacteria. This may be an uncomfortable thought at first but single-cell organisms, bacteria, outnumber our own cells ten to one. On and in us is an entire universe of bacteria that are essential to our health and functioning. Without the bacteria we simply wouldn't exist, we have grown to need each other. The epicenter of this bacteria is in the gut, where there exists a complex bacterial ecosystem that plays a massive role in who and how we are.

Just as the gut microbiome can influence the brain, so too can the brain influence the microbiome. Increased stress can throw the balance off in your microbiome, making you more susceptible to illness and disease. The two 'brains' almost work in tandem, communicating with each other in an effort to keep the overall system in equilibrium. This new wave of research may provide new ways of treating disorders like anxiety and depression using healthy probiotic bacteria. Treating the microbiome in order to treat the brain. Scientists now know that 95% of the body's supply of serotonin, a neurochemical responsible for good mood, sleep, digestion, and other functions, is manufactured by gut bacteria. Anyone's attempt to live a healthy and balanced life without taking care of their gut microbiome is attempting in vain. Further, if you're trying to build a fortress of mental strength, with the ability to handle the obstacles and the stressors of everyday life, you cannot underestimate the effect that gut health has on your physical, emotional, and psychological well-being.

A Healthy Microbiome for a Healthy Brain

The gut is the only organ that has its own independent nervous system. That means that there are millions and millions of neurons inside the gut, just as there are neurons inside the brain. Our guts are sterile when we're born, and developing the bacteria that we need in our gut is a normal part of the developmental phase. We need all that bacteria to help break down food into nutrients and protect the gut walls. Gut bacteria aids the functioning of our immune systems and protects against bad bacteria. The bacteria itself produces neurochemicals that interact with the brain, sending signals and communications. This is why the gut can have such an effect on the brain and body. Because of all the neurons in the gut, scientists have dubbed it the "second brain." Gut bacteria have also been found to use immune cells to communicate with the brain, showing that there may be multiple pathways of communication between the two.

As the bacteria in your gut is so influential, we would want only the positive kinds of bacteria to flourish. For the bacteria itself to be healthy, it needs nutrients to consume. Nutrients are what food is broken down into from food, and so we can aid the functioning of gut bacteria by providing it with the best cocktail of nutrients to thrive. Therefore, when we eat, we are serving our own interests and the interests of our gut bacteria. Food must strike the balance between satisfying our taste buds and satisfying the needs of the microbial civilization in our gut. That may sound silly, but poor gut health can have devastating effects on the body and the brain. Poor quality nutrients and dangerous molecules that find themselves in the gut can set your gut microbiome's balance off, leading to poor health. Beyond food, things like stress can tip the balance off, so gut health, much like human health, is holistic. Just as you need to tend to particular cognitive behavior and thought patterns through daily habits such as journaling and mindfulness, you need to make a habit out of tending to your gut bacteria. Your microbiome isn't just a bunch of bacteria separate from you; in many ways it is you. To take care of your gut bacteria is to take care of yourself. Having a healthy microbiome can be one of the most potent preventative measures in avoiding illness, disease, pain, and mental health issues. Microbiome health is multifaceted, influenced by your environment, genetics, medication, and diet. Some of these factors can't be changed, and some are incredibly subjective. What you can focus on at home to improve your gut health is your diet. Luckily, for most people at least, this just involves fine-tuning your eating habits. These eating habits are not new, they're mostly the same types of foods you've been told to eat before and you will have to avoid the same kinds of foods you've been told to avoid before. It's simple, but it may not be easy.

Diet itself can be a loaded word, involving all sorts of negative images of restrictive eating and neurotic tracing of food amounts and nutritional values. Diets are also an extreme but temporary solution to a bigger problem. Thus, eating habits is what you should focus on. It's less about all the things that you can't eat and more about what you should be eating to live a healthy life. Eating good quality food promotes the growth of good bacteria, and a healthy microbiome. Consuming poor quality food promotes bad bacteria and a weakened microbiome. The way you eat also needs to become a sustainable lifestyle that still allows you to enjoy what you eat. Here are some simple guidelines to follow.

You should be eating whole foods that provide the necessary macronutrients for your body to develop and function. Macronutrients simply mean protein, carbohydrates, fats, as well as things like fiber, minerals, and vitamins. If you build healthy eating habits out of food that contains essential macronutrients, you will have to put a lot less effort into adding a long list of foods into your diet and forcing yourself not to eat processed foods. Your habits will do most of the work for you.

You Are What You Eat: Choose Wisely

A very simplified version of what a healthy plate of food looks like is one where half of your plate is made up of vegetables and fruits, but mostly vegetables. Protein makes up one-quarter of your plate, and the final quarter is made up of whole grains. What each of these categories entails for you depends on your preferences, dietary requirements, and resources, as long as the ingredients are whole foods and not overly processed. I encourage you to build each one of your meals using this simple puzzle method once you know what specific foods will form part of your eating habits. Your plate must also include healthy plant oils like olive, and a glass of water. There is a lot of information and misinformation out there regarding healthy eating so I encourage you keep it simple using this plating method which is well researched and developed by the Harvard School of Public Health. You don't need much more than this, unless you have very specific goals or requirements.

So what foods form part of the healthy eating plate and serve to improve gut health? Firstly, foods high in calcium and vitamin D are essential. Calcium rich foods include things like spinach, kale, okra, soybeans, and certain fish like sardines and salmon, as well as the calcium classics like dairy products. Foods high in vitamin D include mushrooms, fatty fish like tuna and salmon, beef liver, cheese, and egg yolks. Fiber is an important component of a healthy meal; things like fruit, vegetables, grains, and beans. Antioxidants are necessary to help fight inflammation. Foods with antioxidants are berries, leafy green vegetables, turmeric, omega-3 fatty acids, and dark chocolate. Folate is a vitamin B that assists in dopamine production, and dopamine is a neurochemical responsible for motivation, energy, and reward. Foods like leafy greens, lentils, and cantaloupes have folate. An important mineral that helps healthy functioning is magnesium, and you can get more magnesium from almonds, spinach, bananas, and beans. Lastly, fermented foods like kimchi, sauerkraut, tempeh, and kombucha are packed with probiotics.

Most of these foods should be forming part of your healthy plate anyways. Some may be a bit more obscure, so you can add it to a meal every now and again or try to find a simpler alternative. Certain supplements may be easier than eating a specific food that you don't enjoy. Some supplements come with the added benefit of increasing levels of dopamine. Probiotic supplements do this, as well as mucuna pruriens and ginkgo biloba supplements. Green tea, caffeine, ginseng, and fish oils are also supplements that have been found to increase dopamine. Again, avoid over-complicating this process. If some of these foods and supplements feel too complicated, expensive, and cumbersome, don't worry about them too much. An easy approach is just to ask your local green grocer for seasonal greens or fruits. This holistic yet wholesome approach will ensure you are able to get your hands on the freshest, seasonally affordable edible nutrients possible. Focus on the basics until the habit develops, then let the habit become second nature. If you want to start getting fancy and experimental, wait until the simple habits are running on autopilot.

Remember that the main thing you should be limiting is processed foods, specifically chemically processed foods. These are foods with artificial flavors, colors, and sweeteners that have very little nutritional value. These foods are sometimes called 'cosmetic' foods. Foods you should be including in your eating habits are whole foods, food with as few artificial additives as possible. It is difficult to find foods that are not processed at all, and are entirely organic, in today's world of mass food production. But there are some obvious red flags; frozen or pre-made meals, baked goods, breakfast cereals, chips, sweets, carbonated drinks, most fast-food restaurants, and reconstituted meats (sausages, fish fingers, nuggets). If you enjoy a treat every now and again, then by all means indulge in your favorite snack. Sometimes all you need is to enjoy a slice of cake on a birthday. However, these foods shouldn't be part of your eating habits, they should be rare exceptions. The lack of nutritional value and bad bacteria that comes with processed and sugary foods will only hurt your overall well-being.

Get Moving for a Brighter Mind

Stress, anxiety, and depression affect millions of people around the globe at increasingly higher rates than ever before. Treating these issues has become a major public health concern and, as information has become easier to access, more people are actively trying to find solutions in their personal lives. This has also given rise to wealthy and powerful pharmaceutical companies that provide an array of medications for the treatment of mental health struggles. Although there is a growing distrust of these companies and their medication amongst the public, many people have seen a significant improvement from medication. In extreme circumstances, health professionals advocate for a multifaceted approach involving a combination of medication on top of various forms of therapy and other treatments. In less extreme circumstances, and in circumstances where someone isn't particularly struggling with poor mental health but simply wants to ensure that they are healthy and happy, there is a very simple triad of factors that can have a massive impact on one's health. These are food, sleep, and exercise.

Eating a balanced diet consisting of nutritional food, getting sufficient and good quality sleep, and exercising regularly are core to your overall health. Because they seem so simple, many people neglect them and focus their attention on loftier solutions. Food has been dealt with above, and there is plenty of research and resources on the importance of food and how to eat healthily. Sleep has been mentioned throughout this book and has also seen a resurgence in the scientific literature as people are discovering more about why we sleep and how to get better sleep. Exercise will then form the bulk of this discussion. The effects of exercise on your physical health are well known at this point; increased lung capacity, better cardiovascular health, strengthening of muscles and joints, and more. But exercise is a treasure trove for those seeking to improve their mood and brain functioning. Regular exercise can improve energy levels, sleep quality, and memory, while reducing stress.

Research has found that running for 15 minutes or walking for an hour a day can reduce the risk of depression up to 26% and reduce depression symptoms. This is because research has proved that exercise reduces inflammation, aids in neural growth, and releases endorphins—neurochemicals that improve our mood and energy levels. As an added benefit, the sense of flow or mindfulness that we experience while we are engrossed in physical activities aid in stress reduction by giving us a break from the mental noise. If you need a break to recharge, or you need to hit reset on the stress and tension from work, finding the time for a quick bout of weightlifting, jogging, boxing, or whatever physical activity you enjoy, should be a no-brainer. Even better than cure, though, is prevention. Exercise can give you all of the above benefits on a regular basis, and reduce the risk of developing mental health concerns.

Exercise can greatly improve your self-confidence too, especially if you are starting to feel and see progress. It leaves you feeling stronger, fitter, and more capable. If you feel better about yourself, you are more likely to use more positive words and think positive thoughts about yourself. This goes back to the earlier chapters regarding mindfulness of the language you use and how it shapes your reality. Exercise holds benefits for all people of all ages and fitness levels. The key is to work at your own pace, and gradually push yourself as you get fitter and stronger. In choosing what exercises to incorporate into your routine, focus on what you enjoy as you don't want to have to force yourself to do something you hate every day. Be cognizant of your schedule and the level of free time you have. It would be self-defeating to choose an activity that requires a lot of time to complete when you only have limited free time, and you may end up just feeling guilty that you can't make it work.

Figure out if you want to exercise in a group or alone. Perhaps your work has some kind of exercise club, or perhaps you prefer to go to the gym early in the morning in solitude. A good starting point is to exercise for 20-30 minutes, three times a week. Think about trying yoga, walking around your neighborhood, jogging, gardening or yard work, or tennis at a local club. There are so many excuses to be active. It may seem laborious to go exercise on top of what may be a very busy schedule, but remember your goals when you picked this book up. If you want to improve your mental strength, you need to take as many steps as you can toward that goal. You need to finetune your environment to create the conditions for happiness, confidence, and health. Don't think about how difficult your exercise may be, or how it's taking you away from your work. Think about how good it feels to be active, how grateful you are that you can be active, and how much healthier you'll be in the long run.

Demi Lovato: Combatting Stress One Punch at a Time

Another example of a celebrity who has used their platform to normalize the conversation around mental health is Demi Lovato. They have struggled with eating disorders and self-image for some years, which was a difficult thing to manage while being in the spotlight as a Disney star. While other additional forms of therapy were necessary for Demi, they found that exercise was a central part of their recovery. Their exercise helped build strength and fitness which had a hugely positive impact on their self-image and confidence. Beyond the physical benefits, exercise helped Demi relieve some of the stress and the negative and toxic thoughts, and it helped them with balance. They tried a lot of different kinds of exercise, but found that yoga and running on a treadmill wasn't doing it for them. Instead, combat sports have become their bread and butter; jujitsu, boxing, and Muay Thai.

They still sometimes struggle to find the time to exercise regularly with a busy schedule. This will be true for many people reading this book, often there is one thing that dominates our lives, and we end up with little free time. That's why it's important to prioritize exercise. Make the time for it because it's so important for your health. Exercise, as with many things, is about balance. Demi warns that if it starts to feel like a punishment then you should stop. It's important to develop a healthy relationship with exercise. Know that it is good for you, even on days when you don't particularly feel like going. But accept that sometimes you will fail. Just as easily as exercise can be good for us, it can become bad. People can become obsessive over their exercise by overtraining and feeling excessive guilt every time they miss a workout. It's all about balance.

Strong Takeaways for Tough Times

- Exercise and diet are critical to how you feel throughout the day. When you exercise, your body secretes chemicals known as endorphins, which help to reduce your perception of pain and promote positive feelings.
- Eating balanced meals made up of whole foods is the best way to get all the necessary nutrients and promote good gut health. After all, a healthy gut microbiome is essential to a healthy brain and body.
- Make time in your day for exercise as it can help reduce stress, reduce the risks of depression and anxiety, keep your body healthy, promote sleep, and improve your self-confidence.

Weatherproof Mind Practice #7: Focus on Your Fuel

Food and exercise both influence the way chemicals in our bodies react. If you consume the right fuel, it can clear your mind and boost your energy, while processed foods can lead to us feeling lethargic and drained. Likewise, when you exercise, the endorphins that course through your body will make you feel stronger, happier, and more confident. Focus on your fuel to transform your body and mind.

• Try reducing the amount of fried and processed foods like fries and cold cuts you consume and replace that with fruit and vegetables. Within days, you will start to feel the difference as the increase in nutrients starts to improve your wellbeing.

• Choose one type of exercise that appeals to you if you don't already exercise, it could be something simple like a 15-minute walk around the block during your lunch break or after supper, it could be a 10-minute HIIT (high-intensity interval training) that you can follow on YouTube, cycling or even lifting weights in your garage. Try it today, and believe me, after a week you will feel the positive change in your body and mind.

In the next chapter, we'll dive into another kind of activity that's key to boosting your mental health and resilience: meditation, and why it's a daily vitamin for your soul.

Chapter 8:

MEDITATION: REDUCE STRESS & FIND CLARITY IN THE NOW

Your goal is not to battle with the mind, but to witness the mind.
–Swami Muktananda

The earlier chapters have consistently mentioned meditation as a tool for self-awareness, stress relief, gratitude, and more. This chapter will explore more of the nitty-gritty of how meditation works and why it's so good for you. It's important to stress that meditation should become part of your routine, not just something you do as a cure for stress and overwhelm. Consistently practicing meditation, much like all of the other habits in this book, builds up your resilience and confidence and gives you the coping mechanisms to handle a VUCA world. If you are pressed for time, then start small by setting aside 10 minutes of every day for a quick meditation. Alternatively, you can practice mindfulness using the techniques described in this chapter, most of which are regular daily tasks.

Why Meditation Is
Your Vitamin for the Mind

Meditation is one of those fascinating practices that have been an essential component to many human cultures for thousands of years, before there was any ability to empirically measure the effects it has on your brain and body. But, as it was increasingly put to the test using scientific methods, irrefutable evidence spoke to its health benefits. There are many things that humans don't do anymore because we realized just how unhealthy they were, or that they simply no longer served a purpose. Meditation has made it through the scientific revolution unscathed, if anything it has emerged stronger because we as a society place so much emphasis on evidence. Still, that isn't to say it is an easy thing to do or master. Some religious and spiritual figures perfect meditation over decades of practice, eliciting effects on the brain similar to those of high dosage psychedelic drugs. The goal here is to develop a consistent practice of being aware of your thoughts, which can be achieved by anyone at any level with consistency.

Meditation can have impactful benefits on the brain. Think of it as your body's daily multivitamin for your brain. It can increase levels of serotonin production, resulting in reduced stress and risk of depression. Serotonin is a particularly important neurochemical, contributing to good mood, and an increase in serotonin helps the brain produce more brain cells. Meditation also decreases cortisol, the chemical responsible for stress. Our bodies under stress produce cortisol and adrenaline which are released into the bloodstream. In certain circumstances, this is absolutely necessary, and we have evolved to rely on that stress for survival. But many of the dangers that we evolved to avoid, such as predators and the natural environment, aren't things we deal with now. Our brains, however, continue to feel stress and they can interpret all of the daily stressors like work, traffic, social media, and anxiety as threats in the same way they used to interpret lions and thunderstorms as threats. Meditation and mindfulness can reduce cortisol levels by up to 50% according to one study, and other studies have consistently shown similar effects.

Dehydroepiandrosterone, or DHEA, is a naturally occurring steroid hormone released by the adrenals that play a role in the health of many different components in the body such as bone density, skin quality, muscle mass, and libido. Its general anti-aging qualities are why it is referred to as the longevity molecule, and as we age, we experience a decrease in DHEA production. Meditation can boost DHEA levels by up to 40%. In a similar vein, meditation can boost growth hormone production. Growth hormone aids in muscle, bone, and skin growth as well as tissue and organ health. We experience a gradual decrease in growth hormone with age resulting in weaker bones, muscles, organs, increased fat, and fatigue. Exercise has been touted as the main endorphin-inducing activity, but meditation has been shown to boost endorphins more than running. Endorphins are responsible for putting us in a good mood and giving us a feel-good effect.

Meditation can also boost melatonin levels, the hormone responsible for sleep, and the sleep cycle. Our sleep cycles have evolved to be dependent on light, and the pineal gland in the brain releases melatonin as it gets darker. However, in today's world, we are saturated with light coming from bulbs, screens, streetlamps, and appliances. Our natural melatonin levels have thus suffered. Research has found astounding increases in melatonin levels in those that meditate. Beyond the brain, meditation has been shown to increase our sense of connection to others which, if combined with a group meditation session, can increase our social connections. NFk-B, a protein complex involved in inflammation, can be lowered through meditation and thus inflammation can be reduced. This reduction in inflammation as well as meditation's effect on calmness makes it a powerful pain reliever.

Meditation Is Not Just Sitting There

The benefits of meditation go on, including strengthening your immune system, reducing anxiety, improving mood, increased compassion, attention, and focus. These effects have all been found through research on meditation. However, the research often involved participants meditating regularly or meditation specialists. It would be unrealistic to assume that upon meditating once for 10 minutes that you will experience every positive consequence simultaneously. It requires patience and practice. So how exactly do you incorporate meditation into your routine? One of the most traditional ways is to find a quiet and comfortable place to sit, use a meditation app if you are a beginner, relax your body, focus on your breath, and observe your thoughts as they appear and disappear. This is practiced by most meditators, and is a great way to get comfortable with stillness and quiet. But it isn't the only way.

Some people may prefer to be active while meditating, or they may not have enough time to set aside 20 minutes for meditation and 20 minutes for a walk and 20 minutes to clean the dishes so they need to double up. Walking meditation may be the answer.

This form of meditation can still be done using an app if you prefer. The main goal is to be aware of your surroundings and bring your attention to your breath while observing your thoughts, emotions, and sensations. If you need to tend to your garden and find time to meditate, try combining the two. Simply being outdoors decreases our cortisol levels, so when you are being active in nature and meditating, both activities that decrease stress and improve mood, it can be a potent combo. Again, the goal is to be aware of your surroundings, the sights, sounds, and textures, while bringing your attention to your breath.

If you enjoy partaking in creative and artistic activities, try combining these with meditation. Adult coloring books have seen a boost in popularity and they're a great excuse to practice mindfulness. This isn't surprising as art therapy has and remains a well-established form of therapy. Research has found that coloring in patterns while practicing mindfulness can decrease anxiety. Coloring and tracing involve passive thinking which quietens down the busy thought-centers of our brain, allowing us to be present. Another creative way to meditate is through knitting and crafting. For knitting, the rhythmic and repetitive nature can be deeply calming. Knitting and crafting alone can have positive effects on stress relief and calmness, so throwing meditation into the mix wouldn't hurt. If none of the above ways appeal to you, find another activity that allows you to practice mindfulness and focus on your breath. Experiment until you find what suits you best.

Combining meditation and exercise is always a good idea. Some types of exercise, especially martial arts, already contain a component of mindfulness in them. Try tai chi, karate, boxing, or a form of dance. See if these allow you to remain mindful and calm. Hobbies could be the perfect meditation practice. The next time you're playing guitar or building model cars or making pottery, be intentional about focusing on your breath and observing your thoughts without getting attached to them. Try this the next time you're cooking, especially when you're cooking a healthy meal. It's good to connect with your body and appreciate the nutrients you're giving it. Prayer may be the best form of meditation as your focus is directed at one single thing. Or if you practice any particular ritual or ceremony, try to add in an aspect of mindfulness next time. Cleaning, scrubbing, showering, folding, or any activity you need to do around your house can be an excuse to practice mindfulness.

Tips for Better Meditation

Whether you've just begun your meditation journey or you've been practicing meditation for a while now, you may feel like it's still an awkward and laborious process. You may struggle to get into the groove and feel like there are distractions waiting around every corner. Here are some simple tips to assist you. Firstly, focus on your senses. Let the sounds, sights, smells, and textures around you in. This will give you a better sense of your surroundings and ground you in the present. As you let the senses in, you will start to notice more: distant sounds or obscure smells. Next, focus on the energy of your movements. Meditation may look a certain way to us, or if we are doing active meditation that activity may look a certain way. Forget about doing the activity correctly and focus on the movement itself. Think of it as focusing on the intention behind the movement, the mind's connection to the body that drives the movement. It may take some time to feel that mind-body connection, but it helps you remain present.

All of the benefits to meditation traced above are not guarantees. No one can tell you with 100% certainty that you will experience every positive side effect and that your depression, anxiety, and stress will disappear. Rather, they are likelihoods based on evidence. It's important to approach meditation with as few expectations as possible. The motivation behind meditating should be to get to know your mind better. Whatever else happens is a fortunate bonus. As this is about habit forming, it's best to choose a time to meditate and stick to it. This will allow meditation to become an entrenched part of your routine, and maybe even second nature. Try 10 minutes before you journal at the end of the day, or 1o minutes while you're making lunch. To the same point, pick a location to meditate in and stick to it. If you are trying to do everything in one room or space, it becomes increasingly difficult to transition from one activity to the next. Create as much of a calming environment as you can in one corner that becomes your meditation space.

A recurring theme in this book is creating the best conditions for a particular goal. Broadly speaking, daily habits create the conditions for mental strength, but even within the smaller individual habits, it's necessary to create optimal conditions. Jumping straight from work or exercise into a meditation session is not the most conducive. You're more likely to struggle to concentrate and get into it. Instead, take some time to wind down and prepare. Stop working, walk to the kitchen, drink a glass of water, look out the window or just focus on the water you're drinking, take a few breaths, and slowly make your way to the meditation space. This gives you a break to refocus your intention on your next activity. If your meditation time is at the end of the day, do it after you've finished work and exercise, you've eaten, showered, brushed your teeth, and are preparing to go to bed. You've now created a sufficient buffer between your busy daily activities and your meditation.

To really make sure you have taken the time to wind down between activities, take a few deep breaths to ground yourself in the present before you start the actual meditation. Deep breaths trigger a relaxation response that counteracts the fight or flight mode we may be in after a long day. Breath is important throughout the meditation, and you should continuously bring your attention back to your breath. When a thought arises, notice it, acknowledge it, and bring your attention back to your breath again. Be kind to yourself. Some days will be more difficult than others and there will be a range of factors that determine this. Don't think of it as your fault or failure when you struggle to get into a meditative state. Importantly, notice your emotions while you meditate. The process of noticing and acknowledging your thoughts may give rise to certain emotions. Notice and acknowledge those too. It's all part of the process of self-awareness. To make this an easier process, try out a guided meditation app that does the bulk of the instructive work for you. That way you just do what it tells you to do. If you don't want any more apps, try a meditation class with an instructor.

Ray Dalio:
Find Clarity Amid Volatility

The kind of hustle culture found in Silicon Valley and Wall Street is commonly associated with high intensity, no days off, and at times ruthless work ethic. This kind of work ethic may bring you the kind of success and wealth that you are looking for, but it alone doesn't bring you balance. That's why some in the upper echelons of society have been vocal about how they get balance and maintain their calm. One such person is Ray Dalio, billionaire founder, co-chief investment officer, and co-chairman of the world's largest hedge fund, Bridgewater Associates. Ray is an advocate for transcendental meditation, a particular kind of meditation that revolves around repeating a particular mantra over and over again. Ray credits much of his success to his daily meditation practices, which he does twice a day for 2o minutes each.

Ray says he finds a quiet place, sits down, closes his eyes, and concentrates on his mantra. With transcendental meditation, people often go on courses where they learn their personal mantra which they don't share with anyone, but you can also repeat the syllable om for practice. After a period of repetition, the mantra eclipses your thoughts and feelings and you get into a transcendental mind state, hence the name. Ray does his meditations right after waking and before dinner, which he says helps clear his mind and help him make better decisions. Meditation can help anyone, in any profession, and at any level of success to clear their minds and enhance decision making. Some proponents of transcendental meditation say that it allows you to tap into the creative parts of your brain, increasing creativity.

Strong Takeaways for Tough Times

- Meditation is a daily vitamin for your soul. Just like how our body creates endorphins that lift our mood when we exercise our body, when we meditate, we exercise our mind. This in turn produces essential neurochemicals and hormones that promote health and longevity.

- You don't have to meditate in the 'conventional' manner in order to be 'meditating.' There are many ways to practice active meditation that may suit you better.

- Meditation isn't just a tool for relieving stress but is also a way to start learning about focusing on living life in the moment, without being weighed down by self-imposed expectations and stressors.

Weatherproof Mind Practice #8: Find Your Flow

Meditation is really just a practice that helps you enter a state of flow so that you only focus on the present moment. While finding 10 to 15 minutes to sit still in a quiet spot is great, this practice admittedly does not have the lowest threshold and will require practice just like anything else. That is why I wanted to help you focus on the core principle behind meditation – finding your flow and enjoying your glow during this state. This can be done in many other ways:

• First, decide if you prefer quiet or active meditation. On the quiet side, this could be anything from listening intently to slow instrumental music, knitting, or building a model. For active meditation, this could be walking intently, practicing an instrument, or trying tai chi or yoga. These activities all enable you to enter a state of flow.

• Now schedule one specific time in your daily schedule where you can engage in this activity and practice your meditation every day, even if it's just for 5 minutes to start. You will start to feel the benefits even after a few sessions.

In the next chapter, you'll discover the power of visualization and how it can help you achieve your goals while building your confidence.

Chapter 9:

THINK ABOUT THRIVING, PLAN HOW YOU WILL SUCCEED

If you want to reach a goal, you must 'see the reaching' in your own mind before you actually arrive at your goal.
–Zig Ziglar

efore you can thrive, you need to know where you want to arrive. Working towards that destination gives meaning and purpose. It keeps us motivated and energized. When we know where we want to arrive, we can start to paint a picture of what it looks like. Visualization is a deeply personal and effective way to program the very picture of success you want for yourself. The beauty of visualization is that it takes place in your head and is thus entirely your own creation. An important part of the entire journey that this book aims to set you up for is knowing what you want and what you value. Knowing what your idea of success is, unshackled from any external expectations and influences, is a form of freedom. It steers you away from jobs, company, and habits that don't serve you. We will likely still have to endure some hardship in the form of a difficult job, uncomfortable company, and demanding habits, but once we know that they are in service of our ultimate picture of success they will be infinitely easier to cope with.

The Value of Visualization

Visualization depends on and enhances the mind-body connection. Your mind's power to influence the body is a potent yet often untapped ability. Research into visualization shows that those who visualize a particular activity or practice can actually change their body's physiology. Participants in one study who were tasked with visualizing their workouts experienced an increase in finger abduction strength almost to the same degree as those who completed the workouts. This is largely because visualization activates the same areas of the brain as is activated when the actual exercise is being done. Our minds have extraordinary power to shape our reality. Many top tier athletes use visualization techniques before they practice or perform, and it has become a common component of the sports world since its introduction by the Soviets in the 1970s.

Science continues to show just how visualization works. Mental imagery activates many parts of the brain that are active when you complete a specific movement; motor control, attention, and perception. Thinking about doing an activity initiates the same mental instructions as doing the activity. Therefore, mental imagery is a brilliant way to train your body. But visualization has benefits beyond physical exercise, it has been found to increase motivation, confidence, and self-confidence. Picturing yourself doing anything can then be a way to prime yourself and find motivation to do that thing. Visualization can work for your professional goals just as easily, as you picture yourself completing a task given to you, getting a promotion, or receiving an award. Visualization can assist you in your personal goals, helping you to run those 10 miles, jump that extra 3 inches in height, finish the last three chapters of your book, or talk to the cute stranger that you always see at the bookstore.

The things we want in life can be prepared for through visualization. We do this by imagining the desired scenario in our heads, creating as detailed a picture as we can, engaging all five senses to completely immerse ourselves in the situation, and playing out the exact outcome we would like. It's almost like rehearsing for the real situation. the situation itself may not play out exactly as you imagined, as there are factors beyond your control, but you aren't arriving unprepared. You are confident in your ability to get what needs to be done, done. Building as realistic a scenario as possible is important. Focus on your five senses. Notice the smell in the air, notice the smell you're wearing, the color of your shirt, the position of your body, the music playing through the speakers or the birds chirping, or the footsteps all around you. The picture is yours to paint.

By preparing us for the events, visualization can calm us down. We won't be as surprised by all the external stimuli that confront us in the real world. A significant aspect of anxiety, perhaps the biggest aspect, is uncertainty. When we don't know what will happen in the future, we struggle to make sense of things. This leads to a cascade of physiological responses like sweaty palms, cortisol release, and lack of breath. We can't get rid of that uncertainty because we don't know what will happen in the future. But what we can do is prepare for what we want to happen. When we feel slightly more prepared, we're less hung up on the uncertainty. Visualization helps us feel like we have prepared for the situation. Even though our uncertainty hasn't gone away, we've just run the scenario in our heads so many times that we know what we're aiming for. You may try to visualize all the possible outcomes so you're aware of what could happen.

When you are practicing your visualizations, sit with a straight spine and in a neutral position. You can practice your visualizations at night or first thing in the morning, just like your meditation. You might want to combine the visualization with your meditation or try out a mantra that you repeat similar to transcendental meditation. Your visualization and mantra need to fill your mind, leaving no room for doubts. This allows you to focus entirely on your goal and filter out any extraneous information. You're picturing the place you are trying to arrive at and what it looks, smells, sounds, and feels like. This is what is called outcome visualization. There may be another kind of visualization that works better for a goal that involves many steps. This is called process visualization, where you picture every small step in the process such as regular habits. You may want to try both, depending on the specific goal.

How to Visualize to Thrive

As visualization works off mental imagery, it may be a good idea to start your visualization practice with something you have already experienced success in. If you have already run a marathon before, think back to how good it felt to run across the finish line. Use that emotion to picture yourself running the next marathon that you're training for. This will help you ease into the practice and give you a basis with which to visualize new goals. Intentionality is essential to visualization; thus the clarity of your mental picture needs to be well developed. Work out the specifics of your goal, what it is you want, and why. A vague mental picture of success and happiness is unlikely to manifest in any kind of real behavioral change. Is it a new business strategy that you are about to present to your partners? Are you looking for more emotional honesty with your friends? Do you want to reach a certain weight in the next three months?

The action plan is to visualize, then contextualize. Explore the key elements of this picture of success that you have created and break them into smaller steps that you can achieve. If that is possible, focus on taking those small steps and achieving small wins that will build up your self-confidence. When you do this over and over again, a habit forms. The habit develops a particular state of mind and, when done enough times, these become self-reinforcing. The neural pathways that are activated in this process are similar to a muscle, the more you work them, the stronger they become. Visualization became a regular practice amongst athletes and sportspeople, but as athletes and sportspeople moved into the mainstream and themselves became more popular, so did visualization. Soon, visualization spread to actors, artists, business people, and beyond. Below are some stories of people who have harnessed visualization for their success.

Idris Elba:
When Visualization Becomes Belief

Idris Elba is currently one of the most beloved actors, starring in critically acclaimed and widely praised films and television. Idris began his career, however, near homeless and unemployed. He was struggling to get an acting gig and was about to return to

England from the US. He kept himself focused on his goal by visualizing himself in the same position as some of his favorite actors like Denzel Washington and Wesley Snipes. Idris would visualize himself collecting awards and getting big roles. He was preparing himself for when it eventually happened. He stayed committed to his craft even when it seemed like he was going to fail, all because he had the image in his head, and he was going to make it happen. He believed that he could do it because he saw himself doing it.

Arnold Schwarzenegger: Visualizing Progress

Now cemented as the most famous and one of the most successful bodybuilders of all time, Arnold brought bodybuilding to the mainstream and helped the sport reach new levels of popularity. He did this because he had one of the most impressive and outstanding physiques the bodybuilding world had seen. He achieved this feat, in part due to his use of visualization. He had an idea of the body he wanted, and he visualized that body constantly. This could be described as outcome visualization. However, he also adapted his visualization as he made small progress, showing the use of process visualization, too. Either way, he created a vision and worked towards that vision. Arnold says he used the same technique in his acting and political career.

Oprah Winfrey: Painting Pictures of Success

Oprah began visualizing from a very young age, watching her grandmother work herself to the bone. She kept thinking that her life won't be like her grandmother's, almost as a form of negative visualization. Oprah would also concentrate on thinking that her life would be better, and then the image of that better life began to form. Oprah achieved this better life as one of the biggest and most successful television moguls. She continues to use the visualization technique and couples it with positive affirmations and vision boards. Oprah advocates for this approach on her show and encourages people to aim for their highest selves.

Lindsey Vonn:
Simulating Competitive Scenarios

A great example of visualization as a means of mental practice is Lindsey Vonn. Lindsey is one of the most successful skiers of all time and always visualizes her course before she does it. She imagines every turn, gradient, and bump. This helps her remain calm as she gets ready to do the course for real, as she has practiced many times in her head. Lindsey doesn't just imagine the course in her head though, she shifts back and forth and practices her breathing as if she was simulating it. Visualization also helps Lindsey remember the course, potentially serving as a memory retention mechanism.

Strong Takeaways for Tough Times

- Before you can thrive, you need to know where you want to arrive. Visualization is a way to help you develop as clear an image in your head as you can of what your goal is.

- What you think has a strong effect on how you act. By rehearsing the motions that lead to success in your head, you are increasing the chances that you will follow through with the same motions.

- Opportunity comes to those that are prepared. Focus on filling your mind with your picture of success, and join up that imagery with all of the senses and emotions relating to it. By mentally 'living' the moment, you are framing your mind for success.

Weatherproof Mind Practice #9: Paint Your Picture of Success

Visualization is different from daydreaming. Daydreaming focuses on the outcome and endgame. Visualization is a paint-by-numbers approach to seeing yourself progress towards your goals. It is a very powerful way to internalize your success by mentally going through the motions of seeing yourself achieving your goals step-by-step, with granularity and texture. Going through this process not only helps you paint out the details of what it will entail, it also helps you prepare yourself for the opportunities and choices in life that will give you access to your goals. Why? Because you have rehearsed this in your mind already, and you will be ready to take hold of it.

- Start by taking 5-minutes to try visualizing a goal that you want to achieve for yourself. Find a quiet and comfortable spot where you won't be disturbed during this time.

- Close your eyes and let your thoughts zoom into that goal. If given the right and realistic conditions, how would you achieve this goal? Who and what will you need to work with to make it happen? Get specific, and visualize the images with as much detail as you can muster.

- Take your time to breathe deeply while visualizing your picture of success. When the time is up, you will have started your masterpiece of success. Keep at it until you have full clarity. It's not about making everything perfect; it's about visualizing yourself opening all the doors, and identifying how and where to find the keys to help you do so.

- When you're done, recall the very first step towards painting this picture. Who do you need to connect with, what do you need to do? If you want it, go do it.

In the last chapter, we will explore the importance of achieving a chain of small wins to build self-confidence, and using that momentum to fortify our mind against setbacks.

Chapter 10:

NOBODY'S PERFECT:
AIM FOR QUICK WINS

Nothing builds self-esteem and self-confidence like accomplishment.
–Thomas Carlyle

The Nature of Self-Confidence

Aiming for quick wins allows you to harness the power of progress, and progress helps you feel more self-confident. Self-confidence can be understood as trusting your abilities. But it's more than just self-belief; self-confidence is an energy that is exuded through your thoughts, behaviors, and demeanor. One theory on self-confidence states that it is based on two components: how we feel and what we believe about ourselves, and how well we actually perform. A similar theory states that self-efficacy, a separate but related concept, is based on the belief in future success. Read together, self-confidence relies heavily on the personal belief in oneself. Whether it is a belief in your own abilities or the brief in future success, which are essentially the same beliefs but one is focused on "process", and one is focused on "outcome".

You need to have a firm belief in yourself and the likelihood of success in order to have self-confidence. But that belief may need to be somewhat tied to actual performance. This may vary from person to person as many people have found success through sheer confidence alone, but on average there needs to be a baseline competence for self-confidence to blossom. It may be a chicken or the egg situation to figure out which needs to come first, but it may be practically more beneficial to develop both your belief and your competence. This is because they often feed off each other; belief grows as a result of displayed competence, and competence is put to the test and refined as belief grows. So how do you build your self-confidence? How do you effectively develop your competence and your self-belief in a sustainable way? You focus on quick wins.

The Value of Quick Wins

Focusing our energy on quick wins may be analogous to planting many little seeds, watering them diligently, and having a really good crop yield at the end of a season. You may be tempted instead to plant a massive apple tree because you have the resources and the energy to take care of it then and there, but after a while, you run out of water and space, and it ends up being too big of a project to sustain. At the end of the season, you have no apples and you've squandered valuable resources. Your goals are like the harvest from these crops and apple trees. You need to consistently tend to them and slowly get better at tending to them for there to be anything to show for it over time.

Many people may put this book down, or whatever book they're reading or podcast they're listening to gain important tools for resilience and well-being, and feel so motivated to change and adapt in order to learn these tools that they jump straight into the process. Energy and excitement are amazing to have, and finding the motivation to start the process is sometimes the most difficult part of all of it, but learning the skills in this book takes time. They're muscles that need to be exercised until they work by themselves. Trying to do everything at once can have the complete opposite effect to what we desire and make it easier to become overwhelmed.

Harnessing Progress

When we focus on getting big wins straight away, we recognize that it is an ambitious undertaking. We may even have the self-belief to back it up, but we can often get lost in the milieu of details and moving parts of a big project. This neglects to appreciate the value of progress. Aiming for big wins may seem like progress, you're certainly working hard which must mean you're making progress, right? The thing is, progress can be a finite resource. It's best to make sure that you have a steady flow of it in order to feel like your competence and belief are improving. Some call this the "progress principle": making progress in meaningful work is the single biggest boost of emotions, motivation, and perceptions. Trying to accomplish something too big may inhibit that flow of progress.

The thinkers behind the progress principle were theorizing in the domain of work and the professional world. They were interested in how to keep motivation and productivity up in employees. They found that productivity and creativity depend largely on the employees' experience of emotions, motivation, and perceptions throughout the day. They found that employees with positive emotions, motivation, and perceptions were more productive and were more positive and collegial in their work environments. These feelings and experiences that dictate a worker's positivity and productivity were labeled the inner work-life effect. The intention of this research was to find a way for managers to harness this inner work-life effect. This may be relevant for many readers, whether they form part of the managerial or employee component of their work, but it can and should have relevance to your personal growth and goals, too.

If progress is the largest determining factor in positive emotions, motivation, and perceptions, then we should design our personal endeavors, to the best of our ability, to harness progress. To reiterate, focusing on small wins is a way to experience sustainable progress. Big wins can take time. Hedging all your bets on the rare and large goals that are achieved every now and again is not sustainable. Getting your dream job in a year's time will feel amazing once you've got it, but you won't have a steady trickle of progress throughout the year to build and validate your self-confidence if you're only focused on the end goal. Not to mention that obstacles and unexpected distractions may derail your progress during this pursuit. Building and collecting quick wins is just like collecting medals, and then using them to build a strong defense against criticism and cynical self-talk. The more you build, the stronger you get.

The goal then is not to do away with bigger and long-term goals, but to focus your attention on all of the smaller steps leading up to the big goal. Small, quick wins leave you feeling like you are consistently making progress. If you were to take every daily habit discussed in this book and implement them all at once in order to gain mental strength, you would be a rare breed if you were successful. And if you were, it may take a very long time, leaving you feeling dejected in the process. Identify the goal or goals you want to achieve and break them down into smaller components. Take it one step at a time while you slowly start to journal more regularly, or you make it a whole week without drinking a soda, or you look someone in the eye and tell them you're grateful they made the effort to see you today.

Every one of these little wins is a reason to celebrate your progress. Once you've felt like you've made progress, keep going. Build up your belief that you will reach the next step and the next one after that. With that, your competence at sticking to a routine, self-reflecting on your blind spots in your relationships, forgetting about perfection, and many other habits this book has discussed, will grow. Direct your energy towards accumulating many little successes.

The researchers behind the progress principle note an important aspect of progress and the positive experience related to it: the work must be meaningful. Again, this can be applied to many non-work situations. Of course, it is necessary to find meaningful professional work, and many people have been rethinking what meaningful work is to them, particularly because of COVID-19 and the large-scale social unrest, polarization, and catastrophe. But beyond work, the goals, and the image you are attempting to reach must be meaningful to you. You must want to become a more resilient and adaptable person, you must want to find inner peace and calm, and you must want to live a healthier and more balanced life. If those things are meaningful to you, the progress you make is bound to be more significant.

Quick Wins as a Leadership Skill

We step in and out of leadership roles our whole lives. Whether it is in a sports team, a virtual gaming group, a hiking club, as a teacher, as a father, mentor, project leader, manager, or Imam. There is a time when all of us need to direct a group of people toward a shared goal. Depending on the context and the organization you're part of, this goal may be quite large and ambitious. Just like with your personal goals, it might be tempting to come out swinging with a comprehensive plan to restructure and revitalize on a massive scale. This is especially true for new leaders, who often feel like they have something to prove as they assume their new roles. But chasing this kind of big goal is just as risky in a group as it is as an individual, perhaps more so. When you have a large-scale goal that requires a lot of work, it may happen that the leader takes on the bulk of the work as they feel responsible for executing this plan. What ends up happening is that you don't make space for other people to participate and collaborate.

In a team, one of the most important things is for people to feel like they have made a meaningful contribution. As a leader then your job is to facilitate that. When you get bogged down by details you lose the ability to conduct your team. This happens very often with ambitious leaders. The problem isn't their ambition, it's what they direct that ambition at. If you are not able to become consumed with the details personally, you may still end up micromanaging just to get everything done. Micromanaging interferes with people feeling like they have autonomy, and that their contribution matters. One of the best leadership skills is to do what this whole chapter is about: focus on small, quick wins.

When you break goals into smaller parts, you can more effectively delegate. Each team member will have a job to do and will feel like they have autonomy if they're left to do it. Your team members will feel more valued as they will have made tangible contributions in the form of small wins. The feeling of progress is also important for a team, and it can affect the team's dynamics, synergy, motivation, and more. When the collective feels like they are making progress together, their inner work-life effect will improve. Their emotions, motivation, and perceptions will be far more positive if there is a steady flow of progress. Importantly, this goal that you are working towards must be something that the whole team finds meaningful. Work that isn't meaningful, even if we are making progress, is less likely to improve our emotions, motivation, and perceptions.

Collective quick wins are an important leadership quality, not just to build up that progress and confidence, but because they are shared. Good leaders work towards goals that make their whole team look good. This is what distinguishes leadership from project management. Project management is of course a necessary skill to have as a leader, and achieving quick wins is not possible without effective project management. But a leader is also focused on getting the most out of their team members and making sure that the effort is collective. Leadership is also about creating the best conditions for your team members. Remember the progress principle, and how it is based on emotions, motivation, and perceptions. These things dictate the overall happiness and satisfaction of workers. To be a good leader, you need to enhance those three things so that your team members are as satisfied and happy as they can be.

Even if you're squeezing out all the productivity in your team to produce amazing results, it's not sustainable or even healthy to do that if it is negatively affecting their wellbeing. This may be how many organizations function, to push and push without consideration of wellbeing. Often, there is a culture of high pressure and fear that is used to spur output. You may find yourself with a boss like that, or you may be the boss in an organization that did the same to you when you were coming up. But it is almost always unsustainable. Having a positive inner work life has been shown to correlate with better productivity and satisfaction. At the organizational level, this improves the culture of the workplace. Further, experiencing regular progress improves creative output so it's debatable as to whether overworking your employees for results is even the best method for productivity.

A good leader cares for the team members' well-being as well as the team's ecosystem. To reiterate, happy and satisfied team members are that way largely due to making progress in meaningful work. What meaningful means depends on the team and the organization. Although many people would like to, not everyone's work can fundamentally alter the course of human existence and solve global crises. Work can be meaningful simply because it contributes something to what the worker finds important. Meaningful work can be producing a top-quality product for a customer or fixing something with sentimental value.

Meaningfulness is very subjective, and it falls on the worker as much as it does the leader to find work that is meaningful. As an employee, if you are working a job that will never put you on a project that is meaningful because what they do just isn't important to you, you will struggle to find meaningful work. This is an important aspect of happiness and satisfaction as we are seeing many employees, particularly younger ones, leaving their jobs to find something that gives them meaning. As a separate concept, the search for meaningful work is essential to your overall health and wellbeing. Even with all the mental strength in the world, working a job that gives you no meaning will be difficult.

At the leadership level, in theory at least, the people on your team should find the work meaningful already because they work there. However, even if you are leading a team with members who all genuinely love what they're doing, you still need to make sure they know that their contributions are valued through acknowledgement, support, and encouragement. You can make it easier to achieve team progress by setting clear goals, allowing autonomy, and providing sufficient resources and time. In some ways, you can extrapolate those skills into your own life. When you have made progress, give yourself acknowledgement, support, and encouragement.

Why Quick Wins Feel Good

Building up quick wins helps you get to the bigger wins. You get there through incremental steps and progress. They also provide for a positive feedback loop so we can experiment more with what is working and what is not. There's more room for change when you are trying to take small daily steps. There is also a stronger feeling of control. Control can be a slippery slope, as the tendency to hold on too tight to control can lead to your ego getting in your own way. But resilience is often about finding some kind of calm in the storm, and that calm is the ability to have control over small things in your life. When we feel we have agency, we are more likely to believe that we can complete the tasks we need to and that we have the ability to reach our goals.

Building up quick wins can create a kind of momentum, something difficult to measure but very much felt. As your belief and momentum builds, you will feel more self-confident, and you will want to keep building on your progress. It fights off any feeling of stagnation that you may struggle with if you were stuck on a bigger task.

When your goals require any kind of cooperation, quick wins can build trust and belief. When we focus on a large task and get bogged down by the details, we scramble to feel like we have control. This can result in us dominating the tasks and leaving no room for other contributors. Whether professional or personal, some tasks need to be completed with assistance, and having smaller, more manageable goals allows more people to join in and contribute.

Just as we discussed in Chapter 5, let go of perfection. When you have many quick goals to achieve, you may fail at some. Progress doesn't mean that you achieve 100% of your goals, it just means that you're consistently working towards them. You will have turbulent weeks that will throw your routine off and jeopardize your progress. But you can always build back up, get better, and become smarter.

Mental strength is the ability to keep building even after the castle has broken down, and it's about finding new ways to build it stronger. Quick wins, for the first 30 days of your new action plan, can be the very low hanging fruit. The things you know you can do, do them and count them as your first wins.

How to Work Towards Quick Wins

Select a particular goal you want to achieve in any area of your life. Self-improvement as a broad category may be a good start. Go back to what we worked on in Chapter 2: Knowing Yourself. What are the things in your life that are causing concern or are in need of fortification? Pick three to five things on that list and rank them according to your own priority or urgency. The first thing on that list should be your first goal. Break that goal into smaller steps, and turn those steps into daily practices. Your goal must be crystal clear. Success regarding that goal must be easy to measure. If you are in a group setting, the goal must be something that all group members care about. The win must be achievable within 90 days. The win must also be achievable given your current resources. It's important for your goals to be realistically achievable. The goal must add value to your life, group, or organization. Don't overload your plate with goals. Just because you're breaking them down into smaller pieces doesn't mean that you can't get overwhelmed.

Jerry Seinfeld: Practice Makes Perfect

Jerry Seinfeld is considered one of the greatest comedians of all time who co-created, co-wrote, and starred in what is considered one of the greatest TV comedies of all time, Seinfeld. Jerry has been an active comedian for decades, with many standup specials under his belt. He has continued to work despite the tremendous earnings he made in the late nineties and early 2000s from his specials and his TV show. Hundreds of millions of dollars later, he stands out as one of the most consistent comedians in the game.

To get to that level of comedy stardom, you need a lot of material. Your writing, whether for your own standup, a show, or for other comedians and performers, needs to have the kind of depth of content that can only come from hours of work. To stay on top of his work, and to avoid succumbing to the grip of procrastination, Jerry developed what some have called the "Seinfeld Strategy." This strategy ensured that day after day he would write jokes and improve his material. The Seinfeld Strategy is quite simple. You place a calendar on a wall that contains every day in the year on one page. Then, you take a red pen and mark off the days that you write. The idea is to not break the chain. As it gets longer and longer, you work harder to keep it going. The motivation is simple; to be a better comedian, he needed to come up with better jokes, and to do that he needed to write. Seinfeld's focus on not breaking the chain allowed him to take his goal one step at a time. It wasn't about making sure that every joke was better than the one before, or whether he felt motivated to write. It was just about writing something down every day. The results took care of themselves. It's a great way to break a goal into smaller components and make it a simple part of your daily routine. Again, the task likely needs to be meaningful to you. Trying to do something every day that you despise or feel no attachment to might be soul-destroying.

Jerry harnessed the power of progress and consistency to hone his skills, belief, and self-confidence. This allowed him to reach new heights as a comedian. For you, not breaking the chain can be a great practice to adopt for an important goal of yours. If it's a task you want to do every day, stick a calendar on your wall and start the chain. If it's something you want to do every few days or every week, experiment with your own version of the Seinfeld Strategy.

Strong Takeaways for Tough Times

- Change is not easy, take it one step at a time. Self-confidence is about self-belief backed by a habit of accomplishments. Quick wins are a great pathway to progress because they are accessible and generally don't require a long time to complete.

- It's important that when you're picking milestones for your quick wins that you pick the right one, so choose quick wins that are related to your First Principles and lead toward you achieving what you want in your Driver column.

- Building a chain of quick wins will give you a strong sense of belief that you can make things happen, with purpose, intent, and efficiency, even through tough times.

Weatherproof Mind Practice #10:
Building Your Win Wall

As you've gone through this book, you will have had many opportunities to think about the goals you want to achieve, and more specifically, how to strengthen your drivers, while building up the skills to minimize your stressors. To build mental strength during tough times, you need to have a mental record of success and the confidence of achievement to act as your armor and catapult to drive you forward. That's why I want you to start a habit of building a succession of quick wins. While quick wins may be small in isolation, when you start to build a regular habit of achieving quick wins on a regular basis, your self-confidence will increase, your stress level will reduce because you know you've got what it takes, and importantly, you will have gained the skillset to turn tasks and projects that may once have been intimidating to you into bite-sized chunks.

Start building quick wins, whether they are simple errands on your to-do list, chunks of your project, or pieces of your Picture of Success that you have visualized, each win on your sleeve that you etch is equal to you laying a brick of success to help you build that Win Wall to weather the storm ahead.

I trust you, and believe in you. Start building your Win Wall today.

Conclusion:

ACTIVATE THE MENTAL STRENGTH IN YOU

The journey towards mental strength, arguably, is a simple but difficult one. A lot of what this book has discussed deals with daily habits and practices that you need to incorporate into your life to slowly build up resilience. In many ways, it's about consistency and progress in every domain of your life; emotional, physical, and psychological health, self-awareness, relationships, and career. And it is equally about accepting that you will stumble in the pursuit of this consistency and progress. You will make mistakes in this forging process and that is very much part of the process. If you practice the daily habits and set the intentions discussed in this book, you will have a massive advantage in forging a stronger you. You will have created the conditions for mental strength.

Let's review some of the main takeaways from this book. The world around you can be a deeply stressful and volatile place. Somewhere in the chaos, you need to be able to manage your own life and find peace, instead of being overwhelmed by the chaos. This is why mental strength is so important. It gives us the clear mind we need to make decisions and the motivation to be on the top of our game. One of the most important aspects of this is self-knowledge. Self-knowledge gives us a firm base to build mental strength because we know what direction we want to go in. Knowing yourself, and accepting yourself, allows you to come to terms with what your triggers are. It's also important to develop a better relationship with yourself. Remember that self-knowledge can be obtained through simple daily habits like journaling and mindfulness.

Often, it is through battling your demons or obstacles that you find the success you're looking for. But knowing yourself gives you a potent source of purpose in those tough times. It keeps you working towards your goal, and along the way, you turn your self-doubt into self-confidence. This is a journey that many other people are on, and realizing that you're not alone can take some of the burden off your shoulders. Being in a positive and happy mind state while you are trying to become more resilient and confident is going to make the journey far more valuable. Bringing positivity into your life lets you reframe your reality and your inner thoughts. One of the best ways to invite that positivity into your life is through gratitude. There are many ways to feel more grateful, and you can make some of them like gratitude journaling part of your daily routine. This will make you more aware of the outer world and less in tune with some of the negative self-talk that can break us down.

In developing a better relationship with yourself and silencing the negative voices in your head, accepting imperfection is a potent tool. We can become overly attached to the idea of perfection and it can ruin our self-perception. Perfection can never be attained, it's okay to aim for good enough. The negative emotions that we carry around with us can be corrosive to our lives and our sense of self. Learn to let go. Acknowledge the negative feeling in your mind, accept that it is what it is, a feeling, and then let it go. Don't overthink, don't dwell on should-haves and would-haves. Let. It. Go. Then look ahead because the sun only moves forward. Negativity has a severe effect on our health and well-being and can manifest in very real ways in our bodies.

Moving past that negativity can be done through many of the other habits and lessons discussed in this book.

One of the most important components of health and wellbeing is healthy eating and exercise. The benefits are far-reaching and numerous. Take care of your gut microbiome and in turn, you will take care of your brain. Eating whole foods and getting enough exercise each day is an antidote to mental health concerns, stress, fatigue, low self-confidence, memory, poor sleep, and more. Incorporate meditation and mindfulness into your routine. Not only do they help us know more about ourselves, but they provide a list of tangible benefits to our health and functioning.

Visualization is a vital tool in achieving your goals. It helps you mentally practice your tasks. Develop a clear picture of what you want and visualize yourself getting to every day. Finally, break your goals up into smaller pieces and aim for quick wins. Quick wins make us feel like we're making progress. Progress helps us build our belief in ourselves and our competence. Belief and competence are essential for self-confidence.

Using these tools and daily habits, you will be better prepared for a VUCA world. They take commitment and hard work, but I believe in every single person that reads this book. I believe that you have the ability to change your reality and build a whole new version of yourself. Self-improvement is a fundamental part of the human experience, and you should always be taking productive steps towards it. Productivity doesn't need to mean work all the time, it means taking steps towards your goal. Work when you need to work, rest when you need to rest, and reflect when you need to reflect. All of that is productive.

Go on to carve out your path and never feel like you have to follow someone else's. Celebrate your victories and brush off your failures. Share this journey with other people and surround yourself with good company. It doesn't need to be a solo venture. Lean on your faith, in your God, your higher power, your personal philosophy, or yourself. You get to create the meaning for your own life, so create something worth it!

IF YOU FOUND THIS BOOK INSPIRING, OR THAT IT HELPED YOU IN ANY WAY, PLEASE LEAVE A REVIEW SO THAT MORE PEOPLE CAN ENJOY THE BENEFITS YOU EXPERIENCED.

About the author

Michael Drew is an award-winning senior executive whose twenty-plus-year career has seen him lead businesses and advise board members in North America, the UK, and Asia.

He evolved from being a serial entrepreneur in his twenties and thirties that successfully exited two startups, to rising through the corporate ranks in both the media and investment fields, having worked on billion-dollar transactions for public companies.

As he entered midlife, his constant challenge to balance a demanding career with fatherhood forced him to question his fast-paced 80-hour work week and led him down a mind-expanding path of realization that success can be achieved without drinking the hustle culture Kool-Aid, and maintaining mental toughness to achieve your goals doesn't mean drilling your body and mind to the ground. This understanding, together with the unprecedented waves of disruption we have lived through in the past few years, inspired him to write this book – Be Mentally Strong During Tough Times, so that he could share his findings and learnings with you; and to let more people know that simply changing your mindset can change your world!

References

7 Key Meditation Chemicals: Melatonin, Serotonin, GABA, DHEA, Endorphins – EOC Institute. (2013). Eocinstitute.org. https://eocinstitute.org/meditation/dhea_gaba_cortisol_hgh_mela tonin_serotonin_endorphins/

A Story Of Self-Discovery Eat Pray Love. (2020, August 20). Www.wicz.com. https://www.wicz.com/story/42520419/a-story-of-self-discovery-eat-pray-love

Ackerman, C. E. (2018, July 18). 12 Tips For Building Self-Confidence and Self-Belief (+PDF Worksheets). PositivePsychology.com. https://positivepsychology.com/self-confidence-self-belief/

Adams, A. (2009). Seeing Is Believing: The Power of Visualization. Psychology Today. https://www.psychologytoday.com/us/blog/flourish/200912/seei ng-is-believing-the-power-visualization

Ahlgrim, C. (2018, April 23). Demi Lovato says balancing exercise with her eating disorder recovery is a "learning process." Insider. https://www.insider.com/demi-lovato-healthy-exercise-2018-4

Amabile, T. M., & Kramer, S. J. (2016, June 8). The Power of Small Wins. Harvard Business Review. https://hbr.org/2011/05/the-power-of-small-wins

Bennett, N., & Lemoine, G. J. (2014, January). What VUCA Really Means for You. Harvard Business Review. https://hbr.org/2014/01/what-vuca-really-means-for-you

Berkheiser, K. (2018, August). 12 Dopamine Supplements to Boost Your Mood. Healthline; Healthline Media. https://www.healthline.com/nutrition/dopamine-supplements

Bradberry, T. (2014, October 21). How Successful People Handle Toxic People. Forbes. https://www.forbes.com/sites/travisbradberry/2014/10/21/how-successful-people-handle-toxic-people/?sh=29744cb52a92

Brown, J., & Wong, J. (2017, June 6). How Gratitude Changes You and Your Brain. Greater Good. https://greatergood.berkeley.edu/article/item/how_gratitude_changes_you_and_your_brain

Bruce, D. F. (2021, April 21). Exercise and Depression. WebMD. https://www.webmd.com/depression/guide/exercise-depression#:~:text=When%2520you%2520exercise%252C%2520your%2520body

Buren, M. E. V., & Safferstone, T. (2009, January 1). The Quick Wins Paradox. Harvard Business Review. https://hbr.org/2009/01/the-quick-wins-paradox

Carpenter, D. (2018). The Science Behind Gratitude (and How It Can Change Your Life). Happify.com. https://www.happify.com/hd/the-science-behind-gratitude/

Carpenter, S. (2022). That gut feeling. Apa.org. https://www.apa.org/monitor/2012/09/gut-feeling#:~:text=Gut%2520bacteria%2520also%2520produce%2520hundreds

Cherry, R. (2019, February 22). Camila Mendes Will Convince You to Pick Up Gratitude Journaling. Www.yahoo.com. https://www.yahoo.com/lifestyle/camila-mendes-convince-pick-gratitude-063626859.html

Clear, J. (2013, July 19). How to Stop Procrastinating by Using the "Seinfeld Strategy." James Clear. https://jamesclear.com/stop-procrastinating-seinfeld-strategy

Clifford, C. (2018, March 16). Hedge fund billionaire Ray Dalio: Meditation is "the single most important reason" for my success. CNBC. https://www.cnbc.com/2018/03/16/bridgewater-associates-ray-dalio-meditation-is-key-to-my-success.html

Cohn, P. (2017, February 7). How Venus Williams Overcame Self-Doubt | Sports Psychology for Tennis. Www.sportspsychologytennis.com. https://www.sportspsychologytennis.com/how-venus-williams-overcame-self-doubt/

Cole, N. (2016, October 16). Inc.Africa. Incafrica.com. https://incafrica.com/library/nicolas-cole-7-steps-to-transform-yourself-from-who-you-are-to-who-you-want-to-be

Cole, W. (2018, March 7). 13 Really Good Reasons To Start Meditating Every Day. Mindbodygreen. https://www.mindbodygreen.com/articles/13-really-good-reasons-to-start meditating-every-day/

Corley, T. (2018, July 25). Tom Corley: Here's why most successful people are upbeat and positive. Www.cnbc.com. https://www.cnbc.com/2018/07/24/tom-corley-why-most-successful-people-are-upbeat-and-positive.html

Egan, B. (2021, March 8). Caleb Followill: "I never allowed myself to get too close to people because of the way I grew up." Independent. https://www.independent.ie/entertainment/music/caleb-followill-i-never-allowed-myself-to-get-too-close-to-people-because-of-the-way-i-grew-up-40171948.html

Felbin, S. (2022, January 12). Venus Williams, 41, Is Ready To End "Gymtimidation" Once And For All. Women's Health. https://www.womenshealthmag.com/fitness/a38747216/venus-williams-how-to-gain-confidence-at-the-gym/

Freitas, L. de. (2021, July 20). Emily Blunt on how her stutter helped her become an actress: "It was the making of me." You. https://www.news24.com/you/celebs/international/emily-blunt-on-how-her-stutter-helped-her-become-an-actress-it-was-the-making-of-me-20210720

Gilbert, E. (2022). Eat, Pray, Love: One Woman's Search for Everything Across Italy, India and Indonesia. Readinggroupguides.com. https://www.readinggroupguides.com/reviews/eat-pray-love-one-womans-search-for-everything-across-italy-india-and-indonesia

Gomstyn, A. (2022). Foods for your mood: How what you eat affects your mental health. Aetna.com. https://www.aetna.com/health-guide/food-affects-mental-health.html#:~:text=When%2520you%2520stick%2520to%2520a

Gratitude Definition | What Is Gratitude. (n.d.). Greater Good.
https://greatergood.berkeley.edu/topic/gratitude/definition#why
_practice

Guerra, J. (2019, February 25). Camila Mendes Uses This Gratitude Journal
Whenever She's Stressed & "All Over The Place." Elite Daily.
https://www.elitedaily.com/p/heres-where-to-get-camila-mendes-
gratitude-journal-if-she-convinced-you-to-give-the-practice-a-shot-
16079553

Harvard Health Publishing. (2021, August 14). Giving thanks can make you
happier - Harvard Health. Harvard Health; Harvard Health.
https://www.health.harvard.edu/healthbeat/giving-thanks-can-
make-you-happier

Harvard School of Public Health. (2017, August 16). The Microbiome. The
Nutrition Source.
https://www.hsph.harvard.edu/nutritionsource/microbiome/#die
t-microbiota

Harvard University. (2019). Healthy Eating Plate. The Nutrition Source.
https://www.hsph.harvard.edu/nutritionsource/healthy-eating-
plate/

Hecht, A. (2010, November 17). Top Foods for Calcium and Vitamin D.
WebMD; WebMD. https://www.webmd.com/food-
recipes/guide/calcium-vitamin-d-foods

Hilary Swank: Confidence Comes From Sharing Your Battles. (2015, July
13). Www.yahoo.com. https://www.yahoo.com/lifestyle/hilary-
swank-confidence-comes-from-sharing-your-123669580968.html

Ignatius, A. (2021, December 9). Walgreens CEO Roz Brewer to Leaders:
Put Your Phones Away and Listen to Employees. Harvard
Business Review. https://hbr.org/2021/12/walgreens-ceo-roz-
brewer-to-leaders-put-your-phones-away-and-listen-to-employees

Kelkar, A. (2021, January 10). IMPORTANCE OF KNOWING
YOURSELF. Www.linkedin.com.
https://www.linkedin.com/pulse/importance-knowing-yourself-
atul-kelkar/

Kiderra, I. (2015, November 4). Who's the "Enviest" of Them All? Ucsdnews.ucsd.edu. https://ucsdnews.ucsd.edu/pressrelease/whos_the_enviest_of_the m_all#:~:text=More%2520than%2520three%2520fourths%2520o f

Kim, L. (2019, September 23). Get To Know LinkedIn CEO Jeff Weiner. Incafrica.com. https://incafrica.com/library/larry-kim-get-to-know-linkedin-ceo-jeff-weiner-10-facts-you-havent-heard

Maloney, B. (2018, January 18). The Damaging Effects of Negativity by Bree Maloney. Marque Medical. https://www.marquemedical.com/damaging-effects-of-negativity/

Mani, M. (2017, September 28). 12 Short Stories on Self Realization And Finding Your True Self. OutofStress.com. https://www.outofstress.com/self-realization-short-stories/#2_The_Lion_and_the_Sheep

McDonough, D. (2019, October 24). 4 Ways To Practice Active Meditation If You Can't Sit Still. Mindbodygreen. https://www.mindbodygreen.com/articles/how-to-meditate-without-actually-meditating/

McGill University. (2020, December 18). SKILLSETS. https://www.mcgill.ca/skillsets/framework/self-knowledge

Newman, K. M. (2015, December 31). To Change Yourself, Change Your World. Greater Good. https://greatergood.berkeley.edu/article/item/to_change_yourself _change_your_world

Oldenburg, A. (2013, October 17). Idris Elba recalls being homeless, on drugs. USA TODAY. https://www.usatoday.com/story/life/people/2013/10/17/idris-elba-used-to-be-homeless-on-drugs-playboy/3001397/

Patel, N. (2015, August 31). Your Secret Mental Weapon: "Don't Let the Perfect Be the Enemy of the Good." Entrepreneur. https://www.entrepreneur.com/article/249676

Pennisi, E. (2020, May 7). Meet the "psychobiome": the gut bacteria that may alter how you think, feel, and act. Www.science.org.

https://www.science.org/content/article/meet-psychobiome-gut-bacteria-may-alter-how-you-think-feel-and-act

Perper, R. (2020, July 10). How to be Patient with Yourself and Others in a Changing World. Therapy Changes. https://therapychanges.com/blog/2020/07/how-to-be-patient-with-yourself-and-others-in-a-changing-world/

Razzetti, G. (2019, February 11). Why Good Enough Is Better than Perfect | By Gustavo Razzetti. Fearlessculture.design. https://www.fearlessculture.design/blog-posts/why-good-enough-is-better-than-perfect#:~:text=For%2520a%2520perfectionist%252C%2520nothing%2520%25E2%2580%2594%2520and

Ribeiro, M. (2019, July 4). How to Become Mentally Strong: 14 Strategies for Building Resilience. PositivePsychology.com. https://positivepsychology.com/mentally-strong/

Rider, H. (2020, July 16). Procrastination Is Really Perfectionism. Psych Central. https://psychcentral.com/blog/procrastination-is-really-perfectionism#1

Robinson, L., Segal, J., & Smith, M. (2021, August). The mental health benefits of exercise. Help Guide. https://www.helpguide.org/articles/healthy-living/the-mental-health-benefits-of-exercise.htm

Rodgers, D. P. (2008, December 9). Kings of Leon's Caleb Followill Admits to Struggling With Anorexia. Nashville Scene. https://www.nashvillescene.com/music/kings-of-leons-caleb-followill-admits-to-struggling-with-anorexia/article_7b1d4b01-f38f-5771-9a11-5675f142e1f0.html

Rollins, S. (2020, October 2). The power of visualization: improve your skill by training your mind – Esports Healthcare. Esports Healthcare. https://esportshealthcare.com/power-of-visualization/#:~:text=Visualization%2520is%2520a%2520powerful%2520technique

Rosalind Brewer: Find Your Voice and Don't Be Silent. (2021, June 23). Stanford Graduate School of Business.

https://www.gsb.stanford.edu/insights/rosalind-brewer-find-your-voice-dont-be-silent

Schwantes, M. (2017, September 30). LinkedIn's CEO Just Gave Some Brilliant Life Advice. Here It Is In 1 Sentence. Incafrica.com. https://incafrica.com/library/marcel-schwantes-linkedins-ceo-just-gave-some-brilliant-life-advice-here-it-is-in-1-sentence

Scipioni, J. (2021, December 18). Billionaire Ray Dalio credits his success to 40 minutes of meditation per day — here's how he does it. CNBC. https://www.cnbc.com/2021/12/18/billionaire-ray-dalio-how-transcendental-meditation-helps-me-succeed.html#:~:text=Long%2520before%2520it%2520was%2520cool

Serena Williams's Grand Slam Titles, Finals, Records. (2019). Tennis-X.com. https://www.tennis-x.com/grand-slam-finals/serena-williams.php

Shah, S. (2020, June 11). 12 must-know meditation tips for beginners. Insider. https://www.insider.com/guides/health/mental-health/meditation-tips-for-beginners

Siwachok, E. (2018). Gratitude: Ego's Antidote. The Arbinger Institute. https://arbinger.com/Blog/Gratitude_cln_Ego%27s_Antidote

SJ Scott. (2019, January 12). How To Be More Self Aware: 8 Tips to Boost Self-Awareness. Develop Good Habits. https://www.developgoodhabits.com/what-is-self-awareness/

Smith, J. (2020, May 14). Processed foods: Health risks and dangers. Www.medicalnewstoday.com. https://www.medicalnewstoday.com/articles/318630

Stockmal, M. (n.d.). Gratitude and Ego. Thriveglobal.com. https://thriveglobal.com/stories/gratitude-and-ego/

Strickler, Y. (2016, July 28). Kickstarter's Impact on the Creative Economy. Kickstarter. https://www.kickstarter.com/blog/kickstarters-impact-on-the-creative-economy

Strickler, Y. (2019, October 24). "Can I Do This Job and Still Be Me?" Marker. https://marker.medium.com/the-self-doubt-we-feel-as-ceos-9adcbc7891d

Suchak, M. (2017, February 1). The Evolution of Gratitude. Greater Good. Https://greatergood.berkeley.edu/article/item/the_evolution_of_gratitude

Tabernero, J. (2021, May 19). 13 Reasons Why Knowing Yourself is Important. Cresentella. https://cresentella.com/13-reasons-why-knowing-yourself-is-important/

The Importance of Self-Reflection In A Relationship. (2019, November 27). Creative Souls. http://creativesoulstribe.com/the-importance-of-self-reflection-in-a-relationship/

Thistlethwaite, F. (2014, August 10). Gwyneth Paltrow moans about her "misguided strive for perfection" on cringe-worthy blog. Express.co.uk. https://www.express.co.uk/celebrity-news/497798/Gwyneth-Paltrow-discusses-her-strive-for-perfection

Tinubu, A., Celebrity, M. A., & Published on August 10, 2020. (2020, August 10). Zendaya Says She Doesn't Have Her Anxiety "Under Control Yet." Showbiz Cheat Sheet. https://www.cheatsheet.com/entertainment/zendaya-anxiety.html/

Trapani, G. (2007, July 24). Jerry Seinfeld's Productivity Secret. Lifehacker; Lifehacker. https://lifehacker.com/jerry-seinfelds-productivity-secret-281626

Van Dijk, S. (2021, April 14). How to calm your inner storm | Psyche Guides. Psyche. https://psyche.co/guides/how-to-calm-your-emotions-with-dialectical-behaviour-therapy

Venus Williams's Grand Slam Titles, Finals, Records. (n.d.). Www.tennis-X.com. Retrieved May 24, 2022, from https://www.tennis-x.com/grand-slam-finals/venus-williams.php

Vogel, K. (2022, January 25). Active Meditation: What It Is, Techniques, and How to Do It. Psych Central. https://psychcentral.com/health/active-meditation

Williams, A. (2015, July 8). 8 Successful People Who Use The Power Of Visualization. Mindbodygreen.

https://www.mindbodygreen.com/0-20630/8-successful-people-who-use-the-power-of-visualization.html

Wilson, C. R. (2021, July 22). What Is Self-Knowledge in Psychology? 8 Examples & Theories. PositivePsychology.com. https://positivepsychology.com/self-knowledge/

Wolf, C. (2016, February 2). Gwyneth Paltrow's Perfectionism Drove Everyone Working on Her Beauty Line Crazy. Racked. https://www.racked.com/2016/2/2/10893988/gwyneth-paltrow-glamour-beauty-line

Made in the USA
Middletown, DE
04 November 2024